# The Person Behind the Mask
## A Guide to Performing Arts Psychology

# Publications in Creativity Research
## Robert S. Albert, Series Editor
### (formerly Creativity Research Monographs as edited by Mark A. Runco)

# The Person Behind the Mask
## A Guide to Performing Arts Psychology

by
Linda H. Hamilton

 Ablex Publishing Corporation
Greenwich, Connecticut
London, England

Printed in the United States of America

**Library of Congress Cataloging-in-Publication Data**

Hamilton, Linda H.
    The person behind the mask : a guide to performing arts psychology
/ Linda H. Hamilton.
       p.    cm. – (Publications in creativity research)
    Includes bibliographical references and index.
    ISBN 1-56750-344-6 (cloth). – ISBN 1-56750-345-4 (pbk.)
    1. Entertainers–Mental health.   2. Entertainers–Psychology.
3. Entertainers–Job stress.   4. Performing arts–Psychological
aspects.   I. Title.   II. Series.
    RC451.4.E57H35   1998
    616.89'0088'79–dc21                    97-22316
P                                                CIP

In order to keep this title in print and available to the academic community, this edition was produced using digital reprint technology in a relatively short print run. This would not have been attainable using traditional methods. Although the cover has been changed from its original appearance, the text remains the same and all materials and methods used still conform to the highest book-making standards.

Ablex Publishing Corporation
55 Old Post Road #2
P.O. Box 5297
Greenwich, CT 06830

Published in the U.K. and Europe by:
JAI Press Ltd.
38 Tavistock Street
Covent Garden
London WC2E 7PB
England

# Contents

# INTRODUCTION

When you sit in a darkened theater, you enter a place of make-believe that is populated by characters, music, drama, and dance. A spotlight is there to illuminate without revealing the machinations behind the scenes. It can all seem so effortless. That is, of course, as long as you are sitting in the audience.

The people who walk through my door reveal a different side to the pageantry. As a psychologist specializing in the performing arts, I see the toll that this career often takes on their lives, whether it is living up to a weight contract or facing middle age—in a profession obsessed with perfection. Paradoxically, this same career offers many opportunities for personal growth, especially when performers can meet new challenges and surpass previous limitations. This book looks at the person behind the mask of performance. It explores narcissism and the performing artist.

Why focus on narcissism? Because this attribute can be found in all normally functioning personalities and plays an integral role in what we do and how we feel about ourselves. For the performer, this aspect of self-esteem regulation is on the line in every production.

To aspire to stardom is to lead a precarious existence, where security resides in the moment. Stage fright and euphoria alternate in dizzying waves, physical appearance can be closely tied to self-esteem, and body weight may dictate success or failure. For most performers, obsession and years of training are necessary, entailing the burden of constant repetition, social isolation and reliance on beloved and/or feared teachers who guide the way. As identity and vocation merge into one, the stresses of work can easily intrude on the performer's life. Self-esteem becomes linked to someone else's response and the emotional toll can be costly. In this world where illusion—not reality—dominates, the private self is often an annoying appendage strapped to the instrument of the performer's muse.

In my clinical practice, clients come from a variety of art forms, including comedy, theater, dance, and music. Many of their concerns echo my own experiences on the stage. As a dancer with the New York City Ballet, I too had suffered from insecurities, chronic injuries, and the elusiveness of peak performance. In my role as a psychologist, it became obvious just how pervasive these issues are for other types of performing artists as well. Research into the mental and physical stresses of the profession added to my understanding of the occupational problems of performers. The next step is prevention, which is what this book is ultimately about.

Over the last decade, performing arts medicine has emerged as a unique subspecialty, comparable to that of sports medicine, which deals with the special needs of performers. My own foray into the field began in New York City at the Miller Institute for Performing Artists, serving a diverse population of students, professionals, and retired artists. I have also participated in various conferences on the arts, beginning with the first world conference on arts medicine in 1992, commemorating both Van Gogh's centennial and Mozart's bicentennial.

Besides my clinical practice, lectures, and consultations at different dance schools, there is also my monthly advice column in *Dance Magazine*. The goal is to educate the community about the stresses involved in this profession.

In terms of health care, there are many positive changes in the quality of performers' treatment over the last few years, due to the steady stream of research in textbooks and professional journals that have proliferated in the field. Still, psychology could play a more active role in the care of performers, as it does with athletes, by drawing attention to how this group handles stress, bounces back from disappointment, and regulates self-esteem.

Within the discipline of psychology, there are many schools of thought. However, being an integrative psychologist, I do not confine myself to a particular school or single-theory approach, believing that different techniques can improve the performer's mental health. Still, I have long thought that narcissism, with its noted relationship to the arts, rich theoretical history, and empirical basis in human behavior, could add an important dimension to our understanding of the psychology of performing artists.

Since the American Psychiatric Association gave us the diagnostic criteria for the narcissistic personality disorder in 1980, researchers have developed measures to assess both healthy and pathological narcissism. Many of us were particularly keen to use these tools on artists; yet the results are mixed, with artists exhibiting traits characteristic of narcissism as part of healthy personality and as a pathological entity! Does this mean that the artist is seriously maladjusted, in the process of self-actualizing, or mentally healthy? The answer depends on the specific frame of reference.

Reading through the psychoanalytic literature will provide a virtual kaleidoscope of differing views on the psychological profile of the artist. Traditional analysts commonly see artists as sublimatory neurotics who transfer their narcissism from themselves to their work, hovering on the brink of a serious disturbance. Ego psychologists, on the other hand, emphasize the healthier aspects of the artistic process. They see this group displaying an admirable capacity for achievement and narcissistic gratification. Self psychologists seem to lie somewhere between these two extremes, because they consider the artistic process to be a primarily reparative effort for an earlier narcissistic injury.

Perhaps the most consistent theme among these different viewpoints is that of narcissism. There is also the implication that the artistic process may be therapeutic, as even artists who are described as maladjusted only "hover" on more severe disturbance. It is this continuum between health and pathology that forms the basis for my examination of narcissism's role in the performing arts.

Among the various theorists, Kohut's self psychology speaks directly to the therapeutic benefits of artistic pursuits by addressing, within a theory of personality development, the exhibitionistic and aesthetic components that are the essence of a performing art. For this reason, I refer to Kohut's ideas, as they relate to the performer, as the primary basis for inference and interpretation in the following chapters.

Briefly put, Kohut believed that the child seeks two fundamental types of relationships with early caretakers that express basic narcissistic needs. First, there is a need to display the self's evolving capacities and be admired for them. Ask performers about their childhoods, and they will often tell you how much they loved to show off to family and friends. According to Kohut, this need represents the child's healthy sense of omnipotence and grandiosity. Later, there is a need to form an idealized image of at least one parent and experience a merger with that parent.

Under the best of circumstances, the child is able to convert these two images from a more global and archaic form into something that is complex, resilient, and internalized. This can result from small but increasing parental failures that do not mirror the child or permit idealization. If this conversion does not take place, there will be an aborted developmental process, accompanied by primitive grandiosity or idealization. Rather than seeing these phenomena as a defensive retreat from reality in adults, Kohut believed that this process constituted a fragile opportunity for the revitalization of the self if it was properly cultivated and warmly received. He also believed that the need for relationships and pursuits that reflect the self continue throughout the person's lifetime.

The premise of this book is that the performing arts, by its very nature, is unpredictable, conferring both advantages and liabilities on those who aspire to its aesthetic ideals. I believe that self-esteem is enhanced when the performer's efforts culminate in a sense of mastery, personal direction, and professional recognition from others. However, I am also aware that repeated narcissistic wounds often occur in those who experience rejection, injuries or chronic disappointment.

Consequently, this book covers performers' experiences throughout their entire career-span from selection and training to occupational functioning and longevity.

Besides relying on current research in the field, I do my best to show the human side of performers through personal interviews, clinical vignettes, and extensive case histories, which illustrate common problems in the arts. In each case, patients' names and identifying characteristics have been altered to protect their identities.

The first chapter begins with the intense training regimen that transforms a wannabe into a star, along with the limited chances of success. Talent, desire, and luck, combined with the input from influential teachers, will all play a role in how performers see themselves in the future. An especially touchy subject is body weight and appearance, which is addressed in the second chapter when I look at the strong relationship between cultural expectations for thinness and eating problems. As you will see in the third chapter, families also play a role in the performer's self-concept through their investment in the gifted child. Therefore, we will examine the behavior of stage parents, as well as the manner in which conflicts from the family of origin get repeated with other authority figures (e.g., teachers and artistic directors) and colleagues.

The fourth chapter focuses on the performer's stage persona and discrepancies between the real and ideal self in the pursuit of perfection. A major source of insecurity in students and professionals often lies in the wish to please significant others. This leads us to the lifestyles of performers in the fifth chapter and factors associated with occupational injuries and retirement. Retiring from an artistic career often strikes at the heart of the performer's identity, instigating a prolonged period of mourning.

In the sixth chapter, I conclude by reviewing psychology's place in the new field of performing arts medicine and the role of mental health in treating work dysfunctions in this population. In much the same way that psychological factors have been incorporated into programs in sports, they could also find a similar role in performing arts academies and companies, eliminating various forms of occupational stress. It is my hope that the information in this book will be useful to performers, teachers, and health care professionals who work in this unique community. Here is a book for those who want to see the person behind the mask.

# 1

# Training Considerations for Performers

The desire to entertain others often begins spontaneously—with a flair for showmanship or an immediate attraction to an art form. A child may naturally sing and dance, engage in role-playing, or tap out melodies on the grand piano (Gardner, 1993; Kogan, 1995). Unfortunately, these precocious performances give few hints of who will make it in this career. Criticism, combined with an arduous course of training, is needed before a "wannabe" is transformed into a seasoned professional. The competition is intense and few ultimately survive.

Because the performing arts are so precarious, I have found that aspiring students who seek out psychotherapy often experience feelings of humiliation, remorse, apathy and lowered self-esteem as they attempt to live up to their earlier promise (Robson & Gitev, 1991a). This chapter addresses training experiences in the performing arts, where the psychologist's challenge lies in helping performers come to terms with personal limitations.

## SELECTION AND SELF-INVESTMENT

While most parents are aware that dancing, playing an instrument, or singing an aria takes a lot of hard work, few understand the personal sacrifices that go along with professional training. My mother enrolled me in ballet at the age of 8, which is standard fare for classical dancers, or for that matter music students who wish to become proficient. Only later did I realize what becoming a professional dancer entailed. In fact, most professionals in music and dance begin training during childhood and continue for close to a decade (Hamilton, Kella, & Hamilton, 1995).

Few students complain. Performing is usually a passion, making the learning process a delight, as well as the growing recognition that comes from family and friends. Still, serious training in the arts is not about being on center stage or prancing about in a tutu. Professional academies require discipline, hard work, and self-denial, basically eliminating students unwilling to invest themselves fully in this vocation. The child who aspires to be a ballerina learns quickly that the mirror is there for corrections—not just to preen! By the time she is 18 years old, she will engage in an automatic inventory of everything that "looks wrong."

As a psychologist, it is obvious that the quality of training often has an important effect on the student's self-concept. In one survey (N=960) conducted for *Dance Magazine*, I learned to my horror that almost half of the dancers had a teacher who unjustly humiliated them in dance class (Hamilton, 1997). While this practice often occurs under the guise of motivating students to work harder, the results were far from satisfactory; these dancers had significantly more performance anxiety, injuries, and thwarted professional aspirations!

Unfortunately, young students have little information about their competencies apart from parental input, teachers' comments, or the reactions of their peers, all of which will have a profound effect on how they see themselves over time. Not surprisingly, some students fare better than others, depending on whether they develop a positive or negative self-concept with resulting high or low self-esteem.

An unusual set of circumstances surrounds child prodigies such as Midori Ito, who began to study the violin at the age of 3, performing at New York's Philharmonic Holiday Gala by the time she was 10 years old. In cases where prodigious talent does not develop in tandem with emotional maturity, children can end up leading an "abnormal" existence, as their world-class gifts are exhibited on a global stage (Press, 1992).

In my work with adults who were the target of this unusual attention, I often discover that their sole sense of their own value lies in being a performer. It is like they are wearing blinders, with little appreciation for other aspects of their evolving identities. As expected, these prodigies are extremely vulnerable, because they do not have additional outlets for recognition and self-expression. Parents also need to guard against handing over their child to an overly harsh or critical teacher. While a nurturing parental relationship contributes to the child's self-esteem (Watson, Hickman, Morris, Milliron, & Whiting, 1995), a destructive teacher can sabotage all of their efforts.

In contrast to such fast-track careers, most aspiring performers spend a large part of their childhood engaging in age-appropriate activities, honing their technique in a classroom with their peers. For some (e.g., opera singers and bassoonists), teachers often postpone this process until puberty when students' bodies are able to sustain the technical demands required by their instrument. Although older students are often better equipped to handle the pressures of training because of their greater maturity, all students need experience on stage through annual workshops and recitals.

Research shows that many cases of performance anxiety develop in students who do not have the opportunity to perform from an early age (Hamilton, 1997). In fact, performing serves as a valuable extension of their training, as long as teachers do not overwhelm children with multiple engagements. I advise parents that each child differs as far as the right amount of scheduled performances and choice of repertoire, so they should exercise care when selecting recitals, competitions, and youth concerts.

Parents and teachers also need to protect children's motivation and self-esteem by focusing attention on their efforts toward mastery, rather than stressing a more performance-oriented goal, such as winning a competition (Roberts & Treasure, 1993). The following case illustrates how problems can arise in young performers who do not learn how to cope with failure:

Case 1.0

The Insecure Dancer

The director of a national ballet company referred an 18-year-old American dancer to me for psychotherapy after a dramatic weight loss of more than fifteen pounds. Although dance critics described her as a rising star, I found that she was fixated on the idea that her talent and admirers could abandon her at any time. As a child, this dancer's teacher had treated her as a failure whenever she made a mistake, constantly comparing her to other promising students. Her insecurity culminated at an international competition when she only got a silver medal, and her teacher rejected her in public. This dancer broke off the relationship, vowing to rely only on her family. Three years later, she saw her first mixed review as a professional because of her maturing figure. A starvation diet quickly corrected the problem, leading to a promotion to ballerina status. The end result is that this dancer now views weight loss as the answer to her pernicious sense of insecurity. In addition to bringing constant concerned attention from others, dieting reinforces her perception of being in control—of her body, if not her talent.

## The Nature of Competition

It goes without saying that children are vulnerable to criticism. Put them on stage, judge them as good or bad, and the results can be disastrous. Fortunately, appropriate teaching can make this situation more benign. According to Carol Dweck (1995), a Columbia University psychologist, children who use an "incremental theory" to evaluate their performance believe that they improve by seeking out new challenges and learning from past mistakes. In contrast, those who go by an "entity theory" see themselves as having a fixed amount of their special gift, making failure particularly distasteful. Training programs that stress the process of learning with its attendant struggles, rather than the illusion of being perfect, help children to explore, take risks, and make mistakes without losing confidence along the way.

It also helps to pay attention to young performers' other talents and interests, because the supply of students in the arts continues to be far greater than the demand. Besides a shortage of adult occupational niches, there are only a limited number of positions in elite arts schools, summer programs, and private classes in the country. The more prestigious the teacher or academy, the greater the level of competition—and the possibility of failure.

The following statistics show just how tough the selection process is for aspiring performers.[1] At the School of American Ballet (SAB), where I began my training, only one-half of the children who audition for 60 openings each year get accepted into the program. Out of this original group, 5% survive the training regimen, which eliminates students based on body shape and technique annually, making it the most competitive program in the country (Dunning, 1985).

A similar experience awaits students who audition for LaGuardia High School to enter its programs in the performing arts and music and art. For the fall semester of 1991, this school received over 10,000 applications; the acceptance rate was 12%, with 8% entering the freshman level.

If you make it this far, can you relax? Not if you want to get a job. Only one out of three (36%) of the alumni from these schools are actively performing five years later[2]—this is after investing most of their childhood training for this career! These poor results are consistent with the United States Census Bureau (1990), which indicates that just 38% of the 354,615 performing artists in the country have full-time work (see Table 1.0).

A steady job in a major company, in my case the New York City Ballet, solves many but not all problems, since union contracts are only renewed on a yearly basis. And the director can also choose not to renew a contract. Economic uncertainty is obvious in the salaries of performing artists, which range between $9,000 and $50,000 annually, and may come from performing a legitimate gig on stage,

TABLE 1.0.   The United States Census Report on Employment and Earnings

| Performing Artist | | # Work at all | Annual Salary | # Work full-time | Annual salary |
|---|---|---|---|---|---|
| Musicians/Composers | M | 63,324 | $16,400 | 31,345 | $31,838 |
| Singers | F | 37,921 | $9,030 | 8,076 | $22,625 |
| Actors/Directors | M | 28,325 | $37,414 | 37,843 | $50,231 |
| | F | 20,783 | $22,843 | 19,449 | $36,941 |
| Dancers | M | 3,431 | $14,578 | 1,267 | $24,378 |
| | F | 11,908 | $11,156 | 3,230 | $19,828 |
| Other | M | 23,991 | $21,377 | 20,295 | $33,570 |
| | F | 28,789 | $11,986 | 14,638 | $24,201 |

*Notes:* The last category includes "Artists, performers and related workers not else-where classified;" M=males; F=females. Based on 1990 statistics.

singing a birthday gram in a gorilla suit, or even more likely, a "survival job" of waiting tables and hoping for the big break.

What, if any, is the solution to this dilemma? Considering the government's current reluctance to support performers through such non-profit organizations as the National Endowment for the Arts, I believe that schools need to prepare students for the realities that await them after graduation. This means learning additional skills, such as word processing, to bring in more money. Practicing time-management is also important to help smooth the transition to another career if this one does not get off the ground. Low-cost health insurance for performers remains a need waiting to be filled on my wish list. However, a promising model is currently being introduced by the Dance Professionals Associates (DPA), which offers cost-effective protection for dancers and their families (see resource directory).

## A Career in the Arts: What is The Attraction?

Given the limited chances of success, many people are surprised at the intensity with which performers identify themselves as members of this profession. Yet neither the level of success nor professional status seem to affect the dedication that characterizes this population (Phillips, 1991; Reciniello, 1991). Instead, it is common for many performers to persist even in the face of chronic disappointment. The question is, why?

Obviously, it is disappointing when work on the stage is not available. Yet many performers use daily classes or auditions as a way to engage in meaningful work and identify with the aesthetic standards of this profession. The motivation to perform is, for all intents and purposes, intrinsic, rather than being based on fame or fortune (Amabile, 1990; Csikszentmihalyi, 1990; Maslow, 1968). "Peak" or "optimal" experiences are also common in this group when skill and challenge combine to produce a pleasing state of euphoria.

In contrast, students with divided attention and goals may drop out of this single-minded pursuit at an early age, since they lack the inner drive to develop one talent to its full potential (Csikszentmihalyi, Rathunde, & Whalen, 1993). Undercommitment in arts students is associated with low self-esteem, a negative self-image, and impaired motivation (Dudek, Berneche, Berube, & Royer, 1991). I also see this problem in performers who fail to thrive even though they love the profession.

Many performers tell me that their work is a large part of who they are as people. Although the exact nature of talent in the performing arts remains elusive, Howard Gardner's work (1993) on multiple intelligences offers a particularly compelling explanation for the origins of domain-specific abilities.

The traditional view of intelligence, which is the basis of current IQ-testing, looks at a certain aptitude as stemming from a single, generalizable "g" factor comprised of verbal and performance components that operate across all domains. Gardner's concept goes way beyond this view, because he speculates that there are really seven different kinds of intelligence, each with strong innate components. Not everyone has them to the same degree, which is why memory and comprehension vary accordingly.

These predispositions affect the manner in which people express themselves and interact with their environment. In the performing arts world, different intelligences appear to support different talents and skills.

For example, kinesthetic intelligence would be a central feature of all performers who must watch, imitate and recreate what is laid before them. As a dancer, I relied on this natural strength by focusing primarily on physical mastery. Yet the "born mimic" who views a scene once, reproducing the most salient features, is also exercising this domain to some degree, as is the musician who uses fine motor control to master an instrument. A musician or singer would excel at the perception and production of music, comprising musical intelligence. Comics and actors, on the other hand, tend to have superior verbal abilities.

Then, there are the personal intelligences. To move beyond technique into the interpretive realm, performers must have access to their emotional life. "Method" acting exploits this ability to turn inward by evoking feelings, expressions, and gestures from a prior time. Performers use the second type of personal intelligence to discriminate the moods and intentions of significant others (e.g., spouse, teacher, director, audience). It is interesting that performers who excel at self-expression are more likely to transmit their moods to others, while receptive artists may catch these feelings through contagion (Goleman, 1991).

## The Lure of Alternative Lifestyles

Along with these natural predispositions, many people believe that certain groups, such as male homosexuals, tend to be artistically inclined (Cooper, 1986). While no one knows whether the incidence of homosexuality is actually higher in the arts (Demb, 1992), many wonder whether this group might be more attracted to an artistic profession. If homosexuals gravitate to the performing arts, is it because of their abilities? Or do they become part of this community because the atmosphere is more tolerant of alternate lifestyles?

A literature search of medical and psychology journals came up with only one study that addressed this issue, but it didn't really answer why homosexuals choose the arts as a profession (Green & Money, 1966). This research involved a longitudinal study on a sample of prepubertal boys, referred by family physicians, educators, and the pediatric clinic of the Johns Hopkins Hospital, because of symptoms of effeminacy.

According to Green and Money, the boys "manifested an exceptional interest in dressing in girl's clothing, avoided play activities typical of boys and preferred those of girls, or stated, overtly, the wish to be a girl." They conducted extensive interviews with the boys and their families, with follow-ups ranging from one to eight years. An unexpected finding emerged: 45% of the boys had an intense interest in the theater with a striking capacity for role-taking and stage acting. The authors described the boys' recreational and vocational aspirations prior to puberty in the following way:

> homosexuality in the theater is by no means due solely to the theater offering such persons a social haven in later years. The path towards acting begins at a time in life when the social acceptance and safety of the theater would not yet be apparent to the boy concerned. (Green & Money, 1966, p. 538)

Still, follow-up showed that the boys did indeed find greater acceptance in school and drama clubs with other artistically inclined individuals, suggesting a mutual interplay between talent and a social setting that offered considerable support.

While debate continues as to whether cross-gender behavior is actually part of a "prehomosexual" configuration (Paul, 1993), it appears that Green and Money's boys' motivation to act stems from their natural talents and abilities. But the question remains—why the attraction to the theater?

In their provocative book, *Brain Sex*, Moir and Jessel (1991) discuss the ramifications of having a female brain pattern in both sexes, based on considerable research from all over the world. According to their findings, women are born with an innate advantage that permits them to display greater emotional sensitivity, receive a wider range of sensory information, and communicate their feelings with greater proficiency. Their interests are also biased toward aesthetic, service-oriented activities. As children, six times as many girls as boys can sing in tune and they have a better visual memory. These "preferred cognitive strategies" may be responsible for the possible attraction of the homosexual population to the performing arts. Hopefully, as this subject becomes less of a taboo, future research will clarify the relationship further.

It appears so far from the findings that performers' deep attachment to their art form stems from a preferred mode of self-expression, based on natural talents and abilities. This, in turn, provides an important source of gratification and self-esteem. Yet it has also been found that giftedness is not synonymous with resiliency, nor are there any guarantees of success. In my work with performers, the teacher, as a guide and potential source of inspiration, often plays a pivotal role in the student's continuing maturation and development.

## THE ROLE OF MENTORING

Most performers have vivid memories of a special teacher during their training. To hone their skills, they need an instructor who will study and critically evaluate them over the course of several years. While there hasn't been much research on the mentoring relationship across different art forms, many former dancers, including myself, found that dancers often see a master teacher as an omnipotent authority figure who is both admired and feared (Forsyth & Kolenda, 1966; Hamilton,

Stricker, & Josephs, 1991). Other health care professionals stress the mentor's crucial influence in the work habits and injuries of young performers (Brandfonbrener, 1991; Freiberg, 1995). In classical music, where students often begin training during early childhood and continue for more than a decade, Ostwald and Avery (1991) have observed that the teacher becomes:

> an extension of parental authority, a sort of "transitional object" significantly influencing the adolescent's developing attitudes in regard to education, career choice, friendships, and even sexual identity. (Ostwald & Avery, 1991, p. 327)

In the worst case scenario, a teacher may even be involved in sexual impropriety, as was alleged in a lawsuit by a former student from the North Carolina School of the Arts (Hamilton, 1995). Subsequently, research found a 16% incidence of sexual harassment in 300 dancers surveyed (Hamilton, 1996). Although one can only speculate as to the frequency of such behaviors in the performing arts, children whose training needs separate them from their families of origin are vulnerable to outside influences.

### Choosing a Teacher

Considering the powerful dimensions of the teacher–student dyad, I am constantly surprised at people who give little attention to the selection process. The reality is that even the best teachers do not serve each student equally well; yet, parents often blindly send their child to train with a teacher based on his or her prior fame as a performer. This is unfortunate, because expertise on stage has little to do with good teaching, particularly in the case of children. Besides raising the question of competency, there may also be a number of unresolved issues about performing, causing teachers to "compete" with their own students.

### Potential Risks

Many problems occur in the mentoring relationship as a result of naivete or poor judgment. For this reason, parents need to learn as much as possible about an art form's training requirements from available literature and informed people in the field.

It is also important to assess each instructor's method of evaluation, hopefully by observing a class. Is the classroom "safe" from public humiliation? Are the teacher's criticisms geared toward a problem-solving approach? If the answer to these questions is "no" then the student would be better off with someone else, regardless of the teacher's reputation in the profession. Again, the quality of the training experience, not the quest for winning at any cost, should be the deciding factor in making the correct choice. The following example illustrates the problems that can develop when this is not the case.

## Case 1.1
## The Rageful Teacher

A widely acclaimed female performer in New York had retired prematurely from the stage following a serious injury. Knowing about her emotional outbursts, which were legendary among people in show business, I was alarmed to learn that she had begun a teaching career and had a reputation for being extremely critical. Unfortunately, her "name" attracted a large following of students, who remained in spite of continued verbal abuse. I got a closer look at this situation when a talented 16-year-old girl from her class came to see me, bearing a striking resemblance to this woman when she was a performer. The teacher had humiliated this student repeatedly, and by the time she sought therapy, she was filled with self-hatred, because she thought she lacked talent. While I was able to help her find a supportive teacher, the emotional damage was more difficult to undo, as she constantly berated herself for even the smallest mistakes. Shortly afterward, this student quit performing. The teacher has since moved on to a prestigious arts program, where she now serves as a guest member of its faculty.

Most performers can recall similar stories of child abuse at some point in their training. The tragedy is that this behavior continues to be practiced under the misguided assumption that pain is necessary for progress. Even if this teaching approach could be justified on technical grounds (which it cannot, given the negative repercussions to this student), there is no excuse for the destruction that these instructors inflict on young performers' self-esteem without regard for the longterm consequences or emotional costs!

Similar to elite sports, aspiring performers are in an extremely vulnerable position when others judge their performance. A belief in their abilities will determine how much of a risk they take. While harsh criticisms are often used to motivate students to excel, they can end up causing more harm than good by diminishing confidence in the performers. Moreover, once low self-esteem occurs, it may seriously impair students' ability to perform up to their potential in the presence of others (Brockner & Hulton, 1978; Richter, Reaves, Deaver, & Lacy, 1982).

Students with high self-esteem, on the other hand, often perform better in front of an audience (Terry & Kearnes, 1993). As a result, training academies should discourage teachers from focusing only on the negative aspects of students' work, or only offering the students open-ended, vaguely defined goals where success is always just out of reach. Otherwise, performers may come to view themselves as lacking in some essential ingredient. Never considered to be "good enough" by others, they may begin a downward slide into a more pathological view of themselves.

### Potential Benefits

Alternatively, teachers who provide a stabilizing influence by instilling values and ideals can increase the students' abilities to cope with the pressures of the profession. The prelude to this developmental process is idealization, whereby students perceive their teacher to be a source of available power. It is during their training that the aspiring performer will (hopefully) learn to approach and meet new challenges, cope with disappointments, and gain a sense of efficacy.

As an antidote to the vulnerability that accompanies this work, a good teacher who stresses mastery over performance can help a student to:

- sustain effort and tolerate moderate amounts of discomfort from mistakes to sore muscles;
- face the boredom and tedium associated with the constant repetition that is required in learning new tasks;
- live with the anxiety that comes from a realistic fear of failure;
- believe that he or she is capable of making progress, as long as this remains within reasonable limits;
- determine when "time out" is needed to prevent injuries and establish healthy work habits;

Under the best of circumstances, the teacher becomes a mentor who serves as a guide without stifling the volition of these gifted young people (Ambrose, Allen, & Huntley, 1994). Instilling trust in the learning process is also essential, because students often respond like children to an important teacher.

In one of my interviews, I spoke with a 36-year-old opera singer who worshipped one teacher, in particular, during adolescence. His words show just how powerful the teaching process can be:

> He was my idol! I admired him and also wanted to identify with him. I tried to understand, not only what he asked for, but why he asked for it. It was like I wanted to be in on the secrets of his mind. At that time, I remember feeling that I needed to be like him in order to be safe. But it was also an ego trip. In other words, if I learn everything he knows, then I can be great too.

As noted here, believing in a teacher's perceived expertise is an important aspect of training in performers, who place these authority figures on pedestals.

### The Mentor as Expert

What happens to performers who work under the tutelage of a legendary figure? In my case, I have to say that when George Balanchine asked me at the age of 16 to join the New York City Ballet, it was a turning point in my life. His death 14 years later, followed by my own career transition into psychology, led me to reconsider my experience from a different perspective.

Balanchine's obituary in *The New York Times* credited him with bringing his art form out of the 19th century and into the 20th, similar to Stravinsky and Picasso. The dance world considered him to be a genius, because his ballets reflected a new type of choreography called neoclassicism, and the dancers who performed them were a new kind of breed—thin, fast, and shaped entirely by him to execute his ballets. When Balanchine died, it was the end of an era, encompassing a remarkable 35 year reign at the New York City Ballet, where he functioned as artistic director, master teacher, and leading choreographer.

Needless to say, his dancers were aware of the power that Balanchine exercised at the New York City Ballet. He had chosen each dancer and was responsible for almost everything that happened on a daily basis—including work schedules, casting, promotions, and retirement. In order to better understand the emotional ties that linked us to Balanchine, I asked 30 dancers from the company a series of open-ended questions, taken from the literature on group processes and the psychosocial aspects specific to the world of ballet ( Forsyth & Kolenda, 1966; Kernberg, 1975; Oskarsson & Klein, 1982). Two years had passed since his death and I was curious to see how Balanchine's dancers felt now that he was gone.

The research used a qualitative content analysis on the interviews to explore repetitive themes and frequently identified issues (Hamilton et al., 1991). Findings showed that most of his dancers (83%) had entered the ballet company during their adolescence, and "grew up" dancing exclusively for Balanchine for an average of nine years. In addition, over half (59%) of these performers felt extremely secure being in the company, which felt like one big family. The rest (34%) told me that company life had a positive impact on their lives, with a small number (7%) reporting it to be ultimately restricting.

Recalling their early impressions, most of the dancers (86%) saw Balanchine as bigger than life, focusing on his power and expertise. This intense idealization continued during their careers, with one-third (34%) reporting a high level of fear intermingled with their awe. Only a few (14%) were struck by this director's more human qualities, whereas the rest saw him as a charismatic figure who had a dramatic effect on their lives. Nearly half of these professionals (45%) felt that Balanchine's guidance released them from personal inhibitions, while the rest felt inspired by his high standards (24%) and pushed to go beyond their previous limitations (28%).

Not surprisingly, Balanchine's praise and criticism had a tremendous impact on his dancers. Two out of three (62%) dancers said that they felt emotionally "high" when he complimented them compared to 38% who actually felt that his praise verified their ability as dancers. Over half of the dancers also considered his criticism to be positive, since it provided useful feedback (31%) and forced them to work harder to gain his approval (28%). However, 31% felt that his critical comments were cruel and basically damaging to their self-esteem. Being overlooked by Balanchine divided the dancers fairly evenly between despondency (48%) and renewed efforts to gain his attention (41%).

What really caught my attention was how child-like the dancers' relationships with this artistic director were, even when they hit middle age. Yet psychologists often seen this in companies where authoritarian leadership, such as Balanchine's, increases dependency and developmental regression. Members assume that security lies in the hands of the leader, idealizing him and making him into a kind of god in the hope of gaining protection (Bion, 1959).

Some psychoanalytic theorists view submission to the expectations of an omnipotent authority figure as evidence of unconscious masochism (Freud, 1963; Kernberg, 1984). However, according to self-psychology, this view bypasses the many benefits that can develop by tapping into this power source, where such surrender offers the potential for further psychological growth (Kohut, 1977). So, did idealizing Balanchine add to these performers' maturation and development?

When I asked about Balanchine's impact, most of the dancers (89%) reported that this relationship had enhanced their lives, continuing to do so even two years after his death. They also said that his influence contributed to their own standards, personal direction, and feelings of self-worth. In contrast, 7% of these performers were unable to connect with him emotionally during their tenure, reporting that their lives had deteriorated since his death. This was the case for one male performer who worked with Balanchine for five years and later retired:

> It's like he was the king and you're a peasant. You don't go near him. That feeling always prevailed when I was around him—of a higher class somehow. If he said "do that step" and I hated it, I'd do it anyway, because he was the master and I was aspiring to this unobtainable nobility. It was a relief when he died. The problem now is that nothing means as much as when he was there standing in the wings.

Idealization of and submission to an authority figure whom one fears or to whom one cannot get close would appear to be the sort of pathological idealization that is unlikely to lead to a greater sense of security, self-esteem, efficacy, and direction. Following Balanchine's death, a small number of his dancers felt depleted and inadequate. Yet more than three-quarters reported a successful alliance, enabling them to absorb this director's magic and charisma plus his technical instruction.

These dancers also continued to benefit from this intense training experience after Balanchine's death. When I asked them to describe the extent to which he was still a part of their lives, most of the responses were typical of this 27-year-old female dancer:

> I guess you'd have to say that he's in every part of my life. In cooking, in dancing, in really making myself beautiful. Even in the way I carry myself. I've started growing my hair long again like he wanted. I read more books, listen to more music, and go to museums because of him. It's become a spiritual thing—knowing he's still there. It just feels much deeper now.

As evidence has shown, the emotional responses that take place in a company are focused on the leader (Kernberg, 1984). In ballet, the teacher–director occupies this role, becoming a powerful figure of authority, due to the dancers' single-minded devotion, early onset of training, and minimal contact with interests or people outside of this profession (Forsyth & Kolenda, 1966). The absolute control that accompanies this position may enhance this perception, as members compete with one another for promotions, recognition, and attention.

Because the mentoring relationship has a significant impact on performers' lifestyle and identity, it is important to take precautions whenever possible to ensure that a teacher is equipped, emotionally and artistically, to handle this responsibility. Psychologists who work with performers should also be aware of the potential problems that exist during training. The mentoring relationship bequeaths a legacy that goes beyond a career, lasting a lifetime.

## TECHNICAL STANDARDS IN TRAINING

Teachers may be the guides to progress but another aspect of training, central to students' self-esteem, is their technique. Performers size themselves up by making social comparisons, self-monitoring, and using mirrors and videotapes. Because this group is notorious for being their own worst critics, it is often difficult to decide whether they have a real technical problem or low self-esteem. Consequently, it is important to take a thorough history of their training. If technique fails to develop according to the art form's requirements, the prospects for a career are bleak—so, it helps to have other options.

For example, many talented dancers who are unable to achieve the 180 degrees of turnout required in classical ballet often thrive in modern dance or musical theater—if given the chance. Unfortunately, performing arts programs often immerse students in a specialized course of training from an early age, bypassing the development of other skills. This leaves aspiring performers with few options other than to drop out of the profession or to feel like failures, which is where mental health professionals come in when they seek out psychotherapy.

One of the performers interviewed for this book remembers her distress at age 17, as her peers began to pass her by in the competitive arena of New York City:

> All of a sudden it's like you're just not good anymore. But it's not because you've stopped trying. I killed myself—I wanted to improve so much. Yet I couldn't get to the next level. The worst part, though, was knowing that it could be done. Other kids were doing it. There you are in class doing your best and knowing that it's the person next to you who's on their way. It's all very confusing.

Sadly, this rude awakening is a fact of life for most performing arts students, except in the case of unusual talent. No matter how hard they try, they may not be able to compete, causing psychological problems in students who lag behind a predetermined ideal.

## In Pursuit of an Aesthetic Ideal

Like other young performers, I remember having role models who seemed to reflect perfectly the standards of my future profession. Psychologists who work with this population need to be aware of these standards, which vary according to each art form (Hamilton et al., 1995; Marchant-Haycox & Wilson, 1992).

In ballet, physical control combines with specific aesthetic dimensions, including long legs, a short torso, and extreme thinness, to produce the proper "line" in a technique that is more demanding than professional football. Few dancers meet all of these requirements.

In contrast, orchestras evaluate classical musicians on their ability to give a flawless performance—not on their appearance. The dilemma here is that nerves and musical instruments are highly unpredictable, and no one is perfect! For vocalists, the demands only seem to increase. I see a number of singers in my practice who struggle with the double "whammy" of weight requirements and a recalcitrant instrument. Besides being rejected if they are heavy, they are often unable to clearly hear their own voices, making it difficult to produce the proper notes or avoid injuries.

Performers may also struggle with gaps in their training, which exacerbate these occupational demands. Many of my clients report technical problems, due to poor instruction at the hands of ill-informed teachers. While retraining is possible, it is time-consuming and emotionally taxing to correct bad habits, particularly if this puts a promising career on hold. Timing also is important. Students who did not have the opportunity to train during childhood cannot play catch-up as adults in art forms such as ballet, a fact that is heartbreaking in the presence of real talent.

Unfortunately, training programs often teach performers that hard work can accomplish anything. Exaggerated perceptions of control are typical of human thought (Taylor & Brown, 1988); still, these can be problematic for aspiring performers. Many students who write in asking for advice at *Dance Magazine* believe that they can do the impossible, such as forcing their legs to turn out (even if they are pigeon-toed). Besides causing serious physical damage, this perception is unrealistic, boxing students into a corner. Students with technical liabilities often need to consider other alternatives, such as a different art form, or something entirely new.

One 26-year-old dancer sought out psychotherapy after a late start in ballet precluded a professional career, leading to considerable emotional anguish and a bout of anorexia nervosa. It was only after years of rejection in ballet auditions, which she was finally able to address in therapy, that she could even begin to consider other options. This performer has since gone into acting, landing two national commercials in the past year, although steady work remains sporadic.

## Confronting Personal Limitations

Needless to say, the illusion that anyone can "make it" in the performing arts is adaptive only if this stays within the realm of possibilities. A positive approach permits the student to work with negative feedback, tolerate ambiguity, and ride the typical peaks and valleys associated with making progress. In order to be truly functional, however, performers must be willing to openly assess their strengths and weaknesses.

For example, a young tenor whose voice is not sufficiently mature to support a Wagnerian opera could have a foreshortened career if he focuses on the illusion of mastery (Duffy, 1991). Likewise, the grandiose actor who believes that she is perfect may be unable to accept direction on a movie set. The degree to which performers can modify these illusions will depend on the dynamics of the personality involved.

## Biases in Self-Perception

How does self-perception work? An interesting study addressed this question in MBA students by asking them to rate their own performance and that of their peers in a managerial group-discussion task (John & Robins, 1994). The researchers then compared the students' assessments to a staff of psychologists trained to observe the group. The results were quite revealing, showing how easy it is for people to delude themselves.

The results showed that students were less accurate when judging themselves than when judging their peers, seeing their own performance in a rosy light, although not too rosy. Individual differences in self-esteem proved to be the deciding factor. Students with high self-esteem, determined by measures of normal narcissism, rated their performance as better than it really was; whereas those with low scores tended to put their work down, diminishing their performance.

It is important to address self-perception biases in psychotherapy when students with low self-esteem fail to recognize their obvious accomplishments. Positive illusions, on the other hand, can be useful up to a point, as long as the student's grandiosity has not exceeded realistic limits.

Of course, performers with serious disruptions in self-esteem have a different set of problems. In pathological narcissism, the person's self-concept fluctuates dramatically, changing from omnipotence to helplessness, egocentrism to low self-esteem, and over-control to a weak identity (Krueger, 1976). In the case of a narcissistic personality disorder, symptoms in the recent version of The Diagnostic and Statistical Manual of Mental Disorders include grandiosity, a need for admiration, preoccupation with idealized fantasies, and severe disturbances in personal relationships (APA, 1994).

Importantly, a more realistic self-concept is related to corrective achievements (e.g., graduation), which is why mastery in the performing arts often leads to healthy self-esteem. A durable relationship and corrective disillusionments that are incompatible with previous grandiosity can also help a person's self-concept, as long as these disillusionments are not accompanied by further rejection (Ronningstam, Gunderson, & Lyons, 1995). A supportive approach with performers would take the form of timely and sensitive comments that highlight their efforts to progress, while pointing out areas that require further work.

## WORK AND IDENTITY

After years of intensive training, performers often have difficulty separating who they are from what they do, as identity and vocation merge into one. Many students sacrifice leisure, social activities, and even certain aspects of childhood to the shrine of this muse. Although the price may seem worth it at the time, a number of elements must still come together before performers reach professional status.

Some performers I have seen in my practice achieve success after great personal cost, whereas others may lose a career from circumstances beyond their control, such as a debilitating injury. Either way, their identities often hang precariously in the balance.

### The Psychological Costs of Talent

Even the most talented students who want to develop their potential must exhibit a single-minded focus, allowing them to work up to an advanced level of expertise. Gifted "drop-outs," on the other hand, are often more socially oriented, which may distract them from the pursuit of one goal (Tomlinson-Keasey & Little, 1990). Training in the performing arts can provide a growing sense of mastery, as well as the esteem-building consequences associated with meeting new challenges. Unfortunately, there is a downside to this passionate interest.

Many aspiring performers inadvertently postpone developmental tasks in adolescence, because they are immersed in hours of daily practice. Consequently, unlike their peers who are experimenting with a variety of roles and identities, work usually becomes the primary means for gaining autonomy, personal fulfillment, and creative expression (Flaherty, 1982; Mayfield & Nash, 1976; Mostow & Newberry, 1975).

A student whose identity is based almost exclusively on performance is less likely to make allowances for the usual disappointments. In these instances, failure to achieve a role in a school recital or gain the recognition of a beloved teacher can be a serious blow to his or her self-esteem.

During psychotherapy, perfectionism is one other common trap for students who fall into an "all or nothing" mode of thinking, which haunts many competitive athletes. They may then magnify minor technical imperfections and practice incessantly, fearing that they will never be "good enough." Students who do not address these problems often have mounting insecurities.

What happens after graduation? Students who learn to doubt themselves during their training often report feelings of inferiority, self-hatred, or a sense of being defective. Frequently, they are unable to cope with the prospect of auditions, withdrawing from tasks that require effort (e.g., a difficult musical piece) or refusing to compete if there is a possibility of failure (e.g., a performance). Other performers may give up after achieving their stated goal to avoid the pressures associated with success. Coping deficits in young performers include underachievement, chronic boredom, and repetitive injuries, as well as the inability to tolerate negative feelings, such as anxiety or frustration.

In cases where more serious disturbances occur, adolescents can fall into behavior patterns that are associated with narcissistic pathology, which Bleiberg (1994) notes include:

> reliance on an omnipotent sense of self, refusal to acknowledge shortcomings and vulnerability, projection of disowned self-experiences onto others, and demands for public affirmation of their power. (Bleiberg, 1994, p. 30)

Importantly, the clinical manifestations will vary, depending on whether one or more of these key elements come to the forefront.

After all is said and done, no one who trains for more than a decade leaves this career without difficulty. Walking away from performing strikes at the heart of the student's self-esteem, leading, in some cases, to a marked deterioration in functioning. A former violinist recalls his depression after graduating from an elite academy only to find himself unemployed:

> After I left my school, I couldn't find work. And I felt like I didn't exist anymore! Music had been my whole life since I was a kid. I loved it so much and I gave so much of myself to it. After five years of struggling, I was all washed up and I hadn't even begun. I went back to school so I could get a "real" job. But I couldn't go to a performance for years. I'm thirty-eight now, but even two years ago, I couldn't believe how much pain I was still feeling. Luckily, I went into therapy and finally got help.

Often, it is difficult to consider other career paths, even after years of rejection and financial hardship. This is the point when illusions of "making it" can be the most maladaptive. In a thorough review of the psychodynamic literature, Taylor and Brown (1988) tell us that:

> a falsely positive sense of accomplishment may lead people to pursue careers and interests for which they are ill-suited. Faith in one's capacity to master situations may lead people to persevere at tasks that may, in fact, be uncontrollable; knowing when to abandon a task may be as important as knowing when to pursue it. (Taylor & Brown, 1988, p. 204)

The emotional and economic uncertainty is a reality for all performers. Yet their passionate commitment to the arts often remains set in concrete. Whether they are avid students, Baryshnikov, or one of the multitudes attending every open audition, they perform because it is more than a job, it is a way of life that can feel as natural and necessary as breathing. The challenge for students—gifted or not—is to find their way through their successes and failures without losing themselves.

Obviously, this is far easier said than done. In my own experience as a professional dancer, it became easier to deal with the ups and downs of this career after I began training for a second career in psychology by taking three courses at Fordham University on my day off from the New York City Ballet. Besides setting a trend (over 35 dancers in the company now take at least 1 college class a semester), my investment in school gave me a valuable source of self-esteem while I danced. Nevertheless, my ties to the performing arts remain an important aspect of my identity today, as they do with so many others in this profession.

In the next chapter, I will discuss another factor that has a significant impact on performers' self-esteem; namely, the "cult of thinness" in society. Just as Miss Universe almost lost her title because she gained weight during her reign in 1996, excess body weight can ruin a promising career in the performing arts.

## NOTES

[1] This information was provided by SAB's registrar, C. Del Corso; the Director of Access and Compliance, L. Edwards, of the High School Division Office of Automated Admissions; and *The Alumni Directory of LaGuardia High School* (1989). New York: Harris Publishing Co., Inc.

[2] The breakdown of former students with careers on stage amounted to 28% from LaGuardia's Performing Arts and 21% from Music and Art. Sixty percent of the dancers from the School of American Ballet performed but only 36% had been accepted into national companies.

# 2

# Weight Standards for the Stage and Screen

Although we all know that physical beauty holds a special fascination in every society (Kogan, 1994), its impact in the theater can literally make or break a career by influencing the audiences' evaluations of both performance and performer. As a result, I find that a negative body image is often connected to low self-esteem, as well as to desperate efforts to conform to current standards of beauty in many performing artists.

Apart from a higher use of cosmetic surgery (Cash & Horton, 1983; Goin & Goin, 1981), the biggest effect of these physical standards is on women who must control their weight. Thinness is now a national obsession, and dieting has reached epidemic proportions (Garner, 1993; Wardle & Marsland, 1990). In art forms, such as classical ballet, the pursuit of thinness is even more pronounced, leading to serious health problems that include anorexia nervosa and bulimia nervosa (Hamilton, Brooks-Gunn, Warren, & Hamilton, 1987). These are not only serious but life-threatening and this chapter examines weight problems in the arts, where cultural pressures to be thin contribute to the onset of eating problems in vulnerable performers.

## DEFINING PHYSICAL PARAMETERS

Who decides how much a woman should weigh? Throughout history, art, fashion and, as always, men's imaginations have helped to define the current ideal in feminine beauty. As a product of the social and cultural context of the times, society then glorifies this body type as a basis for interpersonal attraction—and discrimination.

Today, a thin female figure has become a metaphor for beauty and goodness, influencing the development of countless young girls' personalities and the formation of their self-esteem. This occurs in spite of the fact that physical transformations during adolescence are tied to biological inheritance, resulting in women who come in a variety of shapes and sizes (Stunkard, Harris, Pederson, & McClearn, 1990). Even more perplexing is the quest for the "perfect" body, which is based on an arbitrary standard of beauty. As such, the cult of thinness in Western society is a fairly recent phenomenon.

## Cultural Influences on Weight

In their book, *The Dieter's Dilemma*, (1982) Bennett and Gurin trace the origins of the thin ideal. Emerging after the turn of the century, the thin feminine figure represented a dramatic change in the status of women, which was brought about by a combination of social, economic, and political forces. For the most part, prior to this century, a woman was perceived as not much more than an "instrument" to produce heirs or erotic pleasure for her master. An amply endowed physical ideal portrayed this image with a prominent abdomen, or a narrow waist highlighting bosom and bottom. People considered excess body fat to be beautiful and an economic necessity, because they viewed it as a sign of health, ability to resist disease, and fertility in societies beset with recurrent famines and high rates of infant mortality.

This trend toward a full-bodied look continued into the 18th century, with a few important changes. First, the great famines of Europe had begun to abate after being a regular feature of life for centuries. This led to better nutrition and probably greater fertility, at a time when effective means of birth control had not yet come into common use. In addition, the Age of Enlightenment had opened the door to widespread sexual experimentation and venereal disease was reaching epidemic proportions. The cultural response? It invented the asexual woman, thereby gaining some control over her reproductive functions, as she tortured herself into the latest fashion which included corset and bustle.

The Victorians cultivated this image of a passionless, virtuous, plump yet fertile woman. However, another figure soon appeared in art as a projection of men's fantasies of how a woman would be without inhibitions. This being, known as "femme fatale," or fatal woman, dominated the painting, fiction, theater, sculpture, and opera of the times. What was she like? Men imagined this fatal beauty to be sexually free, childless, more dangerous than vulnerable, and THIN.

## The Thin Ideal in Fashion

By the 1920s women had appropriated the thin silhouette look for themselves, thereby transforming the femme fatale into a less venomous, more acceptable form. Two major changes stand out from this period: the birth-control effort and the women's suffrage movement. Finally unfettered by fat, men, or pregnancy, the new, post-Victorian woman could now be independent with no hint of a reproductive abdomen or voluptuous breasts and hips. It was a time of personal liberation.

The result was a new thin, angular physique that received top-billing in the movies, which had become the most popular form of mass entertainment. Over the years, certain female stars (e.g., May West and Marilyn Monroe) reverted to the more curvaceous shapes of the past, although the thin ideal remained the prototype for women's fashions.

Researchers have documented this switch from the prior well-endowed look in an historical analysis of women's fashion magazines, where they noted few female secondary sexual characteristics during two historical periods—the 1920s and the 1960s and onward (Silverstein, Peterson, Perdue, & Kelly, 1986). With some minor deviations, this thin ideal has continued to dominate women's fashions to the present day's "waif" look.

Besides fashion, research has also shown a shift in cultural attitudes in other embodiments of feminine beauty, such as *Playboy* magazine centerfolds and the Miss America pageant (Garner, Garfinkel, Schwartz & Thompson, 1980). In this survey, the findings showed that the women selected for both *Playboy* and Miss America between 1959 and 1978 were consistently thinner than corresponding actuarial norms for comparable women in the general population. In addition, both *Playboy* centerfolds and Miss America winners and contestants grew progressively thinner over the following 20 years, whereas the average weights of females under the age of 30 increased. What was the cultural response? As women became heavier, there was a heightened attention to dieting articles in six popular magazines. Simply put, if you wanted to be beautiful, you had better be thin.

## The Embodiment of a Mystique

This discrepancy between the thin feminine ideal and physical reality often heightened women's subjective perception of being overweight. The sad fact is that 50 to 80% of adolescent girls diet because they "feel fat," even though the majority are not overweight by objective measures (Attie & Brooks-Gunn, 1989). Society has perverted the quest for thinness into a mystique by conferring it with a special status and a new way of being. According to Bennett and Gurin (1982):

> To be overweight is an aesthetic catastrophe for women, mainly owing to the meaning that has arbitrarily been assigned to it in our culture. The sheer absence of body fat is often perversely interpreted as an asset, but the underlying message is the important one. With her thin body a woman can project a statement about her character: "I am my own sexual boss; I am in control of myself; I am not a motherly, housewifely person." (Bennett & Gurin, 1982, p. 203)

At the close of the 20th century, the only accouterments that have been added to this unrealistic package are breasts and muscle tone (Brant, 1995), which has created an explosion in the number of women who have sought silicone implants (until their recent ban by the FDA) and embarked on a total fitness craze. In the era of AIDS, women are now supposed to "look," although not necessarily *be*, healthy. Far from the original symbol of liberation, today's ideal body has only become another master to be served.

## Women in the Theater

This obsessive preoccupation with body shape and weight is exaggerated in the performing arts. In drama, female actors are often expected to portray an idealized image of physical perfection, based on societal norms for beauty and attractiveness. This can be a particular problem for women when film or videotaping is involved, because there is a tendency to look as much as 10 pounds heavier in this medium than on the stage. Opera singers must also conform to a thinner ideal unlike their role models of the past who (incorrectly) considered plumpness to support the voice. Besides casting that matches appearance with the dramatic aspects of an operatic role, televised productions have also focused attention on the singer's weight.

Nevertheless, it is in the realm of classical dance that the discrepancy between the ideal body and reality reaches its zenith. Although all dancers must be thin, the "look" for females in ballet is essentially prepubescent in shape.

Many of the letters that come to my advice column in *Dance Magazine* are from teenage girls who are desperate to lose weight at any cost. They know that this physical requirement influences dance teachers' evaluations and behavior toward them, peer acceptance in the dance world, favoritism, and their own body image and self-esteem. Every time these young girls scrutinize their reflections in the mirror, they are haunted by this image of perfection. Male dancers have an easier time because they do not face this pressure, as long as they are at their ideal weight for their height.

## THE DANCER'S DILEMMA

From the age of 8, the young dancer is painfully aware that others are judging her on appearance in addition to technical ability. It is no secret to her that her future is tied to her body, which must adapt over the course of a decade according to a set of predetermined physical parameters. At a recent international dance medicine conference in Helsinki, I learned that academies, such as those in China, actually measure their students annually, eliminating all who do not conform to precise physical measurements.

Dance schools may also rely on public admonitions and/or weekly weigh-ins to control the students' weight. In spite of its pressures, rather than creating the desired effect, this authoritarian approach rarely works. Dancers may wear black leotards, stand in front of the "thin" mirror, and get liposuction, but weight fluctuations and chronic concern about eliminating calories are still a way of life.

## The Ideal Body in Ballet

Where did the need to be thin begin in dance? As with fashion, the trend for thinness in ballet is relatively new and has its origins in the Romantic era (Vincent, 1989). Before this time, the roles that dancers performed were rather earthy in nature and required little imagination.

In the Romantic era, choreographers began to create mystical, other-worldly kinds of roles, such as fairies, nymphs, sylphs, and other supernatural beings that appeared to float across the stage, a feat that was best suited to a slender physique. In the 1930s, George Balanchine, my former artistic director, introduced the ultra-thin look to ballet through his neo-classical choreography which streamlined everything from scenery to weight. Since then, his influence in dance has had the effect of intensifying the desire for leanness around the world.

Balanchine told us that we were supposed to look like fashion models—basically tall and very thin. Fortunately, I was one of the lucky dancers who did not need to diet, although some of my colleagues were living on M & M's[TM], cigarettes, and coffee.

Later, I decided to find out more about dancers' weights by conducting surveys of professionals in ballet companies in America, Europe, Russia, and Mainland China and found that most met the same requirements that we did at the New York City Ballet (Hamilton & Hamilton, 1994). Regardless of the country, the average weight for these women hovered at 15% below the ideal weight for their height. Just how thin is this? It is basically the same weight criterion used by the American Psychiatric Association to diagnose anorexia nervosa (APA, 1994).

The ideal body in ballet dancers is in stark contrast to modern and jazz dancers, who do not share the burden of having to be extremely thin. For example, at the American Dance Festival, which is a serious six-week summer program, modern dancers average 6% below their ideal—thin but not out of the question for most women of normal weight (Schnitt, Schnitt, & Del A'Une, 1986).[3] Males, on the other hand, must be physically "fit" in all dance styles but do not have a weight requirement.

Obviously, selecting children with the right bodies is an important key to grooming professionals. Yet many dancers who look perfect at age 8 change dramatically after puberty, which is why competitive dance schools screen their students annually.

While genetic endowment plays a role in maturation, the earlier the dancer begins to train before puberty, the greater the likelihood of a delay in menarche, a characteristic generally associated with a long, lean, linear body (Hamilton, Brooks-Gunn, Warren, & Hamilton, 1988). In contrast, female dancers who menstruate on time (around the age of 12) are more apt to lose the prepubescent shape coveted in ballet. In my private practice, I find many dance students who engage in disordered eating with serious consequences to their health and well-being, because they cannot conform to the ideal body in dance.

## Problems Associated with Poor Nutrition

Many dance schools participate in annual holiday performances, such as "The Nutcracker," or spring workshops that showcase their best students with the thinnest bodies. It is a common practice at this time for dance teachers, who may have poor eating habits themselves, to ask students to "drop" 5 or 10 pounds quickly in order to get cast for a part.

Unfortunately, though, because few dance schools offer nutritional counseling, most dancers have no idea how to lose weight. A 23-year-old dancer who recently came to see me with an eating disorder had started off on her diet at the age of 12 by eating 9 shrimp a day after her school director told her to lose some weight. By the time I saw her, she had multiple health problems and felt guilty whenever she "gave in" and ate a regular meal.

While the previous example is extreme, teachers are known to bypass students for special roles or to criticize them because of their weight—contributing to dancers' negative body-image. Adolescence is already a time of major transition, as young girls begin to integrate changes in appearance, bodily feelings, and reproductive status. In pubescent females, research indicates that body image is more predictive of dieting than maturational status or weight, suggesting that it is a function of transformations of self-representations at puberty (Attie, Brooks-Gunn, & Petersen, 1987). These changes are particularly threatening to dancers, because of the realistic concerns about their careers.

It is not surprising that in an attempt to keep their caloric intake down, dancers often do not eat well. Food faddism, eating to excess and starving, and irrational use of nutritional supplements are common. Consequently, dancers are frequently undernourished and have a number of menstrual problems due to low weights and poor nutrition (Hamilton, Brooks-Gunn, & Warren, 1986). This can be very damaging because delayed menarche and amenorrhea can compromise bone density at a time when adolescents attain 48% of their skeletal mass. Besides hormonal irregularities caused by undernutrition, stress fractures and scoliosis may also occur (Warren, Brooks-Gunn, Hamilton, Warren, & Hamilton, 1986). An example is the dancer who had tried to survive on 9 shrimp a day and suffered five stress fractures throughout her teens, spending approximately four years on crutches with a related injury. An important question is, can anything be done to help young dancers?

After seeing so many of these cases, I contacted the School of American Ballet—the leading dance academy in the country, where I had started my own training at the age of 8. The intervention program that we set up was the first of its kind, with 40 female adolescent students (age = 14.92) who we planned to follow over a three-year period.

Our goal during the first year of this study was to get a baseline of their behavior, followed by interventions in the second year and a one-year follow-up. Because the school director did not want students with problems to go without treatment, we did not use a control group.

The first step in the research was to find out more about these students' nutritional and menstrual habits. The results showed that the dancers' onset of menarche was delayed by more than one year compared to girls who are not dancers, although this delay is similar to that seen in gymnasts (Tofler, Stryer, Micheli, & Herman, 1996). Additionally, 15% had yet to achieve puberty, and 36% had secondary amenorrhea (no menses ≥ 3 months). The dancers averaged 16% below the ideal weight for their height which, if we recall, is an anorexic weight according to the American Psychiatric Association.

As expected, food intake was inadequate: These growing teenagers took in less than 88% of the recommended daily allowance (RDA) for calories in spite of the fact that they were exercising an average of 17 hours per week, while calcium levels were 82% of the RDA. Thirty-three percent of the dancers had scoliosis, which is significantly higher than the 1.6% incidence reported in the general population (Winter, 1986). Ten percent of the sample had experienced stress fractures.

Over the next 12 months, physical problems "weeded out" one out of five of these elite dance students even though all of them had passed competitive auditions to enter SAB. Analyses showed that the drop-outs had menstruated earlier and experienced more major injuries than the dancers who remained in the program. Thus, in addition to losing their prepubescent shape, these students were unable to maintain the rigors of ballet's technique which *is* more demanding, physically and mentally, than professional football (Nicholas, 1975).

In terms of interventions, which included physical rehabilitation, nutritional counseling, and group therapy for eating disorders, it was difficult to say how useful these interventions were because only eight dancers remained in the program. Fifty-five percent of the sample quit dance because of anatomical problems, such as poor turnout which cannot be improved, while the rest found positions in professional companies. Still, even with these mixed results, I believe that dance academies that offer annual screening by a team of health care professionals could help to prevent many problems that arise from the occupational demands of this profession.

Ideally, dancers who survive the training process, graduate, and get accepted into a company are at least suited to ballet's requirements. I, for example, was one out of only four dancers who managed to pass the yearly evaluations at SAB from age 8 to 16, joining the New York City Ballet. To my knowledge, none of us developed eating problems.

Yet many dancers who are not watched so closely manage to become professionals by forcing themselves to lose weight. This research indicates that poor eating habits and injuries continue at the professional level (Hamilton et al., 1986; Hamilton, Hamilton, Meltzer, Marshall, & Molnar, 1989). Unfortunately, weight loss is notoriously unpredictable, and directors may penalize "heavy" dancers (i.e., 4–10%

below ideal weight) with fines and taking away cherished roles or, even worse, their jobs. Our research shows that heavy dancers diet more than thinner dancers (i.e., 11–21% below ideal weight), consuming 900 fewer calories than the recommended daily allowance for active women (1,342 vs. 2,200, respectively). This is 67% of the RDA for calories! Heavier dancers also report more menstrual irregularities.

As a group, dancers with menstrual problems ingest significantly less protein, iron and niacin and report more anorectic and dieting behaviors than dancers without hormonal problems (Hamilton et al., 1986). Dancers' eating habits are also directly related to their concerns about weight; the performers who are terrified of being fat eat significantly less fat, protein, niacin, and iron than those without this concern. They also score higher on questionnaires measuring deviant eating patterns and have more behaviors linked to anorexia nervosa.

### What about Exercise for Weight Loss?

Perhaps the biggest dilemma for dancers is that ballet is not an endurance activity unlike such sports as cross-country skiing, swimming, ice skating, and running. In fact, the exercise characteristics of various forms of dance show that the physical profiles of professional dancers are above those of unconditioned athletes, but certainly not in the league of high-level endurance athletes (Kirkendall & Calabrese, 1983; Schantz & Astrand, 1984).

If you think of it, most variations in ballet last about four minutes; dance training requires only brief periods of low to high level activity that is usually spaced far enough apart to limit an intervening training effect. Because of this, contrary to the layperson's belief, dancing is basically not an aerobic activity and typically expends only 200 calories for women in a one-hour class. Men expend 300 calories but only have to meet their ideal weight to conform to the aesthetic demands of the profession.

The result, compared to male dancers, is that female dancers are often locked in a precarious set of demands. They are required to stay thin in a strenuous discipline that does not burn a lot of calories. Dieting then becomes the main avenue for weight loss.

### The Dangers of Dieting

Dancers often get into trouble when they try to lose weight because the physiological mechanisms associated with dieting can lead to a number of adverse reactions. Researchers believe that these effects, which vary depending on the person, are due to the body's attempts to defend its preferred weight every time a person diets by willing herself not to eat. Nisbett (1972) has hypothesized that a genetic "set-point" for weight exists which determines the amount of fat stored in the body by regulating feelings of hunger, activity level, and metabolic rate. Even though a person's set-point is a matter of many factors, genetic endowment is a significant predictor of that setting.

One of the first studies to examine the contribution of heredity and family environment looked at Danish adoptees and twins reared apart (Stunkard et al., 1990; Stunkard, Sorensen, Hanis, Teasdale, Chakraborty, Schull, & Schulsinger, 1986). The results showed that genetic influences played an important role in determining human fatness in adults, with family-line resemblances hovering at 70%—even if the people grew up in different households! Furthermore, the relation was not confined to the obesity weight class but was present across the whole range of body types—from very thin to very fat. In light of these findings, we now believe that restrained eaters automatically face certain hazards, as dieting is a counterregulatory behavior accompanied by severe psychological distress.

So what happens if a dancer goes on a crash diet? Studies that examine the effects of starvation show a high incidence of episodic binge eating, irritability, depression and, in some cases, psychotic levels of disorganization (Keys, Brozek, Henschel, Mickelsen, & Taylor, 1950). It is important to realize that these results are unrelated to prior psychological adjustment; instead, they seem to arise from attempts to overpower the body's natural level of fatness by resisting its set-point. In addition to setting themselves up to binge, dancers can suffer muscle loss, fatigue, and a marked deterioration in performance. Their resting metabolic rate may also slow down, making it harder to lose weight as time goes by. If the urge to eat wins out (which it usually does) and the performer regains the weight, matters are worsened because there can be a greater percentage of fat because muscle gain is very slow. Furthermore, repeated cycles of weight loss and weight gain (known as the "yo-yo" effect) only make matters worse (Blackburn, Wilson, Kanders, Stein, Lavin, Adler, & Brownell, 1989), because as studies indicate, it can take twice the amount of time to lose the same weight and only one-third of the time to regain it. So, while performers may start out their diets with the best of intentions, the results can be far from the mark and not at all gratifying.

## Competing with the Sylph

Over the last three decades, there has been a dramatic rise in the incidence of both anorexia nervosa and bulimia nervosa in women (Bushnell, Wells, Hornblow, Oakley-Browne, & Joyce, 1990; Eagles, Johnston, Hunter, Lobban, & Millar, 1995; Lucas, Beard, O'Fallon, & Kurland, 1991; Phelps, Andrea, Rizzo, Johnston, & Main, 1993). Important etiologic factors include cultural pressures to be thin, combined with an increase in dieting, apart from more efficient methods of detection (Beaumont, Russell, & Touyz, 1993).

Miss Universe confessed that an eating disorder was responsible for her low weight when she won the contest in 1996. Eating disorders are also high among performing artists, particularly in classical ballet, where the ability to conform to an anorexic ideal can mean the difference between success or failure. During dance training, students have a seven-fold increased chance of developing anorexia nervosa in comparison to their high school counterparts (Garner & Garfinkel, 1980). Competition has particular relevance in this disorder, especially at the level of competition in the different ballet schools. Dancers from more competitive schools have double the incidence of anorexia nervosa—7.6% as compared to 3.5% in dancers from less competitive settings. The authors in this study attribute the higher incidence to greater performance expectations and demands of the more competitive schools.

When the sample at the School of American Ballet was examined, 15% of the adolescent dancers who had auditioned to enter this elite dance academy exhibited a profile consistent with a clinical eating disorder (Hamilton, Hamilton, Warren, Keller, and Molnar, 1997). Surprisingly, these dancers also had significantly more physical deficits, including asymmetries in turnout, leg length and flexibility, as well as greater breast development on the Tanner stages of pubertal development and more missed classes due to injuries.

The dancers' psychological functioning showed, in addition, that they were significantly more depressed, impulsive, maladjusted, isolated, and alienated from their work than dancers without an eating problem. Furthermore, the at-risk dancers saw themselves as failures, felt physically unacceptable, and remained at a below age egocentric stage of development. I believe that dancers who are losing their prepubescent shape and have anatomical deficits may develop eating problems by trying to compensate for their perceived deficiencies in a world that prizes extreme thinness.

Of course, once eating problems have become entrenched, it is difficult to overcome them, even if the student leaves dance. For performers in a professional company, the level of competition continues to be a factor with risks. Another survey evaluated female dancers from eight regional and national ballet companies in America and Western Europe (Hamilton, Brooks-Gunn, & Warren, 1985). Twenty-two percent of the national dancers reported anorexia nervosa, while *no* anorexia was found in the regional dancers. The study also found that national dancers reported their company's standards for thinness were significantly more rigid than regional dancers' companies. As a consequence, national dancers were required to diet more.

Previous work has shown that dancers who are not naturally thin manifest more eating problems in response to ballet's aesthetic demands (Hamilton et al., 1988). Yet not everyone succumbs to these problems regardless of their weight or the professional requirements of performing.

## THE ETIOLOGY OF EATING DISORDERS

Who is vulnerable to a serious eating disorder? Young women between the ages of 10 and 30 are most likely to develop eating problems, which run the gamut from anorexic-like symptoms to full-fledged eating disorders that may even require hospitalization. In the latter case, the prevalence rate ranges from 0.5% to 1.0% for anorexia nervosa and 1% to 3% for bulimia nervosa (APA, 1994). Only 5% to 10% of the new cases presented for treatment each year include men (Hoek, 1993). In weight control programs, binge eating disorders (without compensatory behaviors, such as purging) occur in approximately 30% of this population.

While eating disorders appear to run in families, no one has determined the nature of this component. Still, researchers speculate that the onset of eating disorders is most likely due to a complex interrelationship among personality variables, cultural influences, and genetic vulnerability (Walters & Kendler, 1995).

## Diagnosing Eating Problems in Performers

Assessing eating problems in performing artists is quite challenging because of the realistic concerns associated with weight gain in this profession. As a result, psychologists need to be aware of the physiological problems associated with dieting, such as binge eating, before assuming that the behavior is psychologically motivated.

Compounding the issues, it will also be difficult to make a strict diagnosis of anorexia nervosa in dancers who have amenorrhea and low body weight from stringent dieting, as these characteristics are ubiquitous in this group. Still, a drive for thinness and body dissatisfaction differentiate dancers who go on to develop eating disorders over time and those who don't (Garner, Garfinkel, Rockert, & Olmsted, 1987).

Once the performer's eating has stabilized, it becomes easier to identify the emotional triggers. I make a diagnosis of anorexia or bulimia nervosa according to criteria outlined below in the DSM-IV (APA, 1994). Be prepared, however, to find women who meet most but not all of the criteria in either syndrome. Using self-reports based on DSM-III-R criteria, 46% of professional ballet dancers engage in either anorexic or bulimic behaviors (Hamilton et al., 1988).

## Diagnostic Criteria

Both anorexia nervosa and bulimia nervosa are serious eating disorders that often occur in the same person at different times.

A diagnosis of *anorexia nervosa* is given in performers who refuse to maintain an appropriate weight for their height and age (i.e., less that 15% below ideal), have an intense fear of becoming fat even when underweight and, at times, a disturbed body-image (e.g., they see themselves as heavier than they really are). Weight or shape also unduly influence their self-esteem (or they deny the seriousness of their current low weight), and they have amenorrhea, characterized by the absence of at least three menstrual cycles in postmenarcheal females.

*Bulimia nervosa* involves secretive, recurrent episodes of binge-eating within a two-hour period of time accompanied by a subjective sense of being out of control. The person will then use maladaptive behaviors to prevent weight gain, such as self-induced vomiting, excessive exercise, fasting, or the misuse of laxatives, diuretics, or other medications. A diagnosis of bulimia is given when bingeing and purging occur, on average, at least twice a week for three months.

Psychologists should also be aware that, although anorexia and bulimia nervosa can occur in the same person at different times, they cannot give both diagnoses at the same time. However, the clinician can distinguish anorexics who are bulimic (binge-eating/purging) or restricting types from bulimia nervosa. In the latter case, we type these individuals according to whether or not they purge.

## Underlying Issues

There are several distorted attitudes that underlie an eating disorder. These include the beliefs that one should strive for perfection; self-denial is superior to self-indulgence; fat is disgusting; and weight gain means that you are out of control. These attitudes, which are fostered by the cult of thinness in Western society, offer an avenue for the expression of emotional problems.

Disturbances in personality may precede the onset of eating problems rather than being solely a consequence of these disorders. For example, a relationship exists between body dissatisfaction and a lack of emotional well-being in avid exercisers whose physical appearance is more important to their self-esteem compared to non-exercisers (Davis, 1990). In eating disorders, low self-esteem appears to be a risk factor for both anorexia nervosa and bulimia nervosa even in the absence of major depression (Silverstone, 1990; Walters & Kendler, 1995).

Because self-esteem is so important in the onset of these disorders, there has been considerable speculation about the role that narcissism plays in the development of deviant eating behaviors (Bers, 1988; Goodsitt, 1977, 1983, 1985; Hamilton, 1988b; Thiel & Schussler, 1995). Clinical features most often associated with eating disorders include a primitive defense style, self-devaluation, pathological ineffectiveness (same as learned helplessness), and a precarious sense of self (Bruch, 1973; Garner, Olmsted, & Garfinkel, 1983). These symptoms are commonly found in individuals with narcissistic defects where extreme fluctuations in self-concept are present, ranging from over-control to weak identity (Kreuger, 1976).

## A Psychoanalytic Perspective

Within the psychoanalytic literature, there are three divergent theories that address the development of eating disorders in vulnerable individuals, including drive-conflict, object-relations, and self-psychological points of view (Goodsitt, 1985). Although all of these models address various aspects of eating problems, the latter is particularly useful in explaining the deficits in self-representation of the most disturbed eating-disordered patients.

Self psychologists believe that a disturbance in the parent–child relationship contributes to the onset of eating problems. For example, when the primary caretaker is unable to respond empathically, making it difficult for the child to internalize parental functions that lead to the development of her sense of self (Geist, 1985; Kohut, 1971). Rather than mirroring the child's uniqueness and providing an idealizable model whose soothing presence merges with her own, parental failures in these areas lead to an aborted developmental process.

The outcome can be a lack of self-regulating structures that modulate mood and anxiety and maintain a sense of well-being and security. Instead, the subjective experience of the eating disordered patient is one of fragmentation and helplessness. An actress with bulimia shared her diary with me, graphically describing the emotional anguish associated with this state of affairs.

> God knows what I'm feeling. There was a lot of overeating today. I'm out of control—eating entire boxes of cookies and trying to get rid of them with laxatives or worse, vomiting. Then starting all over. I feel so tired and guilty and wrong. Just terribly out of control and driven. Like a stranger who doesn't own her actions. There's this huge discomfort with being myself. I feel overwhelmed and just want to run away and hide!!!

## Individual Vulnerabilities

For women with serious narcissistic disturbances, focusing on weight with all of its magical connotations may be one way of garnering self-esteem. They may also use certain behaviors to stabilize the self, since eating-disordered patients with narcissistic deficits manifest significantly more obsessive compulsive behaviors than those without these deficits (Thiel & Schussler, 1995).

From what has been said, we should not be surprised that a relationship between eating behavior and pathological narcissism in professional women has also been found (Hamilton, 1988b). In this study (see Table 3.0), women who manifested significant narcissistic disturbances (scores $\geq 10$) exhibited more problems with dieting, bulimia, and oral control than those without this profile. In addition, this group

**TABLE 3.0 Eating Behavior and Narcissism in Professional Women**

|  | Pathological (N=13) | Normal[+] (N=67) |
|---|---|---|
| % Ideal Wt. | −08% | +03%[*] |
| Dieting | 3.60 | 2.90[*] |
| Bulimia | 2.51 | 1.97[*] |
| Oral Control | 2.91 | 2.33[**] |
| EAT-26 | 3.08 | 2.54[*] |
| Real/Ideal Self | 20.38 | 15.69[*] |

Note:  [+]The Narcissistic Personality Disorder Scale (Ashby, Lee, & Duke, 1979); The Eating Attitudes Test (Garner & Garfinkel, 1979); The Ideal Self Scale (Gough & Heilbrun, Jr., 1983); [*] p<.05 [**] p<.01.

was thinner and exhibited a greater discrepancy between ratings of their real and ideal selves, indicating less personal adjustment.

Of course, the degree of disturbance in women with eating problems varies greatly, so it is important to consider this on a case-by-case basis in developing an effective treatment plan. Swift and Stern (1982) have suggested that eating disordered patients can be broadly categorized as falling along a continuum of intrapsychic structure, ranging from borderline personality to identity problems. These subclassifications are useful in selecting the most effective treatment modalities, although there remains considerable heterogeneity in this population (Johnson, 1985).

In practical terms I often consider clients who fall into the most disturbed category to have a borderline personality, which is a variant of narcissistic pathology (Kernberg, 1975; Lowen, 1983). These women are polysymptomatic in nature, making an eating disorder secondary to a more serious problem related to unstructured psychological resources. There is evidence of this disturbance in their life histories, which are generally chaotic and dominated by impulsive behaviors; their mood is labile, fluctuating between rage and emptiness; and boundaries between themselves and others are quite fragile.

During our interview, they often report feeling outside of themselves or depersonalized when binge-eating; purging, in contrast, may help to ward off self-fragmentation. These performers generally respond well to a team approach aimed at life management, involving individual, group, and family therapy. Psychotherapy is highly structured, supportive, and directive rather than insight-oriented, as this approach helps them to feel securely "held."

The next group of clients on the psychological continuum has "false self" organizations, meaning that they are distinguished more by what we do not know about them than what we do know (Winnicott, 1965). These performers are not as disturbed as the former group, presenting uneventful life histories in which their life adjustments appear adequate. The problem is that they are unable to acknowledge feeling needy or dependent. In my initial interviews, they are reluctant to answer questions about food-related behaviors, let alone their emotional needs, as they perceive my inquiries to be overly threatening and intrusive.

A common developmental theme in this group involves premature separation from the mother during infancy, due to a physical or psychological illness or other family situation. In response, they have developed a pseudomature adaptation to life, often feeling as though they are two people; one who is completely in control and another whose infantile needs overwhelm them. Because they fear risking exposure, food becomes their safest and most trusted ally, and it is used to regulate different tension states.

Experience with this group shows me that, although they long for someone to respond to their needs, their self-organization collapses if they acknowledge being needy to another person. Consequently, treatment often involves longterm individual therapy that is relationship-oriented, as they may refuse more directive interventions until we have established a therapeutic alliance. These clients may also refuse to participate in group therapy because they risk exposure.

Identity-conflicted clients fall at the end of this continuum, because most have adequate intrapsychic structure and become involved in food-related behavior for more neurotic reasons. This problem is often conceptualized as part of an adjustment reaction during development, or one that follows clear precipitants, such as moving to a more competitive arts academy. Still, distinctions exist between anorexics and bulimics. In anorexics, the drive for thinness is often tied in with identity and achievement issues, whereas bulimics may use bingeing to compensate for conflicts associated with aggression or sexuality. Identity-conflicted clients respond well to short-term, symptom-focused individual and group therapy that challenges their distorted beliefs, such as those surrounding the pursuit of thinness, body-image, dieting, achievement, and failure.

### Consequences of Eating Disorders

Anorexia nervosa and bulimia nervosa affect virtually every system in the body (Garner, Rockert, Olmsted, Johnson, & Coscina, 1985). Some of the medical complications, such as poor temperature regulation, may be relatively benign while others, including cardiac arrhythmias, severe electrolyte imbalance, and rupture of the esophagus, can be life-threatening. The use of ipecac for self-induced vomiting is particularly problematic, because this substance is easily attained over the counter in pharmacies and is directly toxic to the heart.

Additional medical findings from eating disorders include hair loss, dental decay, palpitations, chest pains, esophagitis, constipation, and anemia. With proper treatment, it is possible to reverse most of these medical complications. Nevertheless, some researchers have found that diminished bone density associated with menstrual dysfunction may persist despite weight restoration. Anorexia nervosa is also one of the few psychiatric disorders that can have an unremitting course that leads to death.

Eating-disordered clients are extremely challenging to treat. Performers with bulimia are often ashamed of their behavior, making any discussion of it taboo until they have "hit bottom" and the silence is broken. Anorectics, in turn, tend to deny the seriousness of the problem, becoming increasingly reluctant to seek treatment as the disease progresses. In the latter case, a concerned family member or teacher will often refer the performer to psychotherapy only after severe weight loss or other signs of malnutrition verge on a serious health risk.

Case 2.0
The Case of Ginger

"Ginger" is a 19-year-old dance student from the Alvin Ailey American Dance Center whose teacher advised her to see me because she was depressed and no longer taking dance class. When she came to my office for her first visit, all I could see was a mass of long blond hair, which she appeared to be using as a shield to keep me away. Establishing contact was not easy with no face in sight, so I took my cues from her body language. Haltingly, in between outbursts of angry tears, she began to tell me her story.

Ginger had been on a roller coaster ride with her weight for most of her teenage years. She was 5'8" tall and had fluctuated between 120 and 150 pounds. At our initial interview, she weighed 140 pounds and was heavier than her peers in dance class. Yet she could not stop eating. From morning to night, she ate everything in sight, particularly sweets and other foods high in calories.

Her eating had been like this for four months, having started after her roommate moved out of their apartment. Because Ginger did not purge, she would stop eating only when she fell asleep from exhaustion, and she eventually gained 20 pounds. She told me that she was now sleeping 12 hours a day, and wanted to "end it all."

As I took her history, I discovered that Ginger's problem with binge-eating had begun when she was age 14 after a dance teacher at a different school told her to lose weight. She had begun menstruating at a normal age and curves were emerging in all the appropriate places, although not for ballet. Ginger began to starve herself and lost a lot of weight until her body eventually rebelled, leading to recurrent binges on the weekend, intense feelings of self-hatred and, eventually, large weight fluctuations.

As we spoke, I realized that the motivation for Ginger's eating problem was tied to her need to regulate different tension states that threatened to overwhelm her. She displayed many of the characteristics of a "false self" organization, as her behavior alternated between apparent maturity and falling apart under emotional stress. After her best friend moved out of their apartment, Ginger acknowledged that it was a minor inconvenience, ignoring the fact that her bingeing had immediately escalated from once a week to every day.

My first therapeutic decision with Ginger was whether to pursue outpatient treatment or suggest that she be hospitalized. Some clients, because of severe emaciation, depression, or multiple binge–purge episodes per day, require hospitalization. At times like this a previous history of treatment failures and medical complications can indicate the need for a more drastic approach.

During Ginger's consultation, it became clear that any of my efforts to establish an outpatient treatment plan were futile because she was completely overwhelmed, unable to function above a minimal level, and severely depressed. She could not stop bingeing and was beginning to feel suicidal, although she had no particular plan. I made arrangements for Ginger to be admitted to an eating disorders unit several days later, where I worked as the head psychologist.

In her hospital treatment, we used a number of techniques, beginning with a full medical evaluation and specialized forms of behavior therapy to help Ginger refrain from bingeing. Individual and group psychotherapy focused on helping her to express herself and to accept support from her peers, while family therapy addressed her premature separation from her parents and a false sense of autonomy.

During our first family meeting, her situation did not appear to be dysfunctional because everyone was very loving toward each other, expressing this in frequent physical demonstrations. The problem was more with how her parents had handled Ginger's vulnerabilities now and in the past. I learned that the message they gave her as a child whenever she became upset was "pull yourself together and get on with it." If she persisted, her mother would decompensate and burst into tears.

Later, I discovered that Ginger's mother had also struggled with depression for most of her life, particularly during her daughter's infancy. Ginger subsequently learned to put on a happy face and hide the turmoil inside. After she moved in to boarding school, this pattern became even more ingrained. Ginger kept her fears to herself, developing a pseudomature adaptation to life's "ups and downs." When she was disturbed, she would head for food—not people—for comfort. This is what happened when her best friend moved out of their apartment.

As her hospitalization progressed, I used cognitive interventions to help restructure Ginger's attitudes toward her food, body weight, and self-esteem. In order to identify the emotional triggers underlying her desire to binge, she kept a diary of her food intake and accompanying feelings. Ginger also met weekly with a nutritionist and engaged in regular healthy exercise. Our psychiatrist treated her depression with a trial of antidepressant medication that improved her mood, allowing her to work more effectively on her recovery. After eight weeks, we transferred Ginger to an aftercare program. Relapse prevention strategies included individual psychotherapy and continuing antidepressant medication. The next step in her recovery was coming to terms with the limitations of her body. Ginger had already given up her dream of becoming a professional ballet dancer; the question now was whether she would live outside of the spotlight or transfer her hopes to another type of performing.

Slowly, she made the transition into acting after a short stint as a modern dancer, which once again aroused negative feelings about her body. I was delighted to turn on the television not too long ago and see Ginger, still with her long blond hair. Only this time, her head up and she looked proud to be performing.

## Treatment and Prevention

Performers need to know about normal changes that affect body shape and weight in adolescence through their schools, as well as understanding adequate nutritional intake. Training academies should also make sure that teachers are aware of the hazards of dieting, and the damage that their critical comments can have on performers' body-image and self-esteem.

It is also crucial to identify adolescents who are at-risk for eating disorders. Major arts academies could offer students annual assessments from a variety of health-care professionals, including psychologists, which could prevent weight-related disorders before these problems start and become a pattern. Calcium supplements and estrogen replacement may also prevent stress fractures when menstrual problems occur.

If weight loss is necessary, students need to follow nutritional guidelines. Daily food intake should not go below 1400 calories or 25 grams of fat; otherwise, the performer may set herself up for binge eating and metabolic problems. Choosing an aerobic activity, such as the stationary bike three times per week, can also make a low weight more attainable. Not only does this type of exercise burn more calories, it is considered to be the only way to actually help lower the body's setpoint.

Finally, it would help if dance schools offered a variety of styles so that girls who are not naturally thin could train in modern dance or jazz in addition to ballet, where a thin body is such a big requirement. Ideally, dance schools could also promote the idea that other career directions are possible and make body weight less of an issue because few students actually go on to become professional dancers.

Although eating disorders are not limited to women in the performing arts, these problems may be exacerbated by aesthetic requirements that foster an unobtainable physical ideal. Psychologists who work with performers need to be sensitive to these vocational constraints.

The next chapter examines the impact of performers' families on their lives. As a microcosm of society, the family-of-origin has wide-ranging consequences in the performing arts, where it influences individual development, career aspirations, and professional relationships over time.

## NOTE

[3] Metropolitan Life Insurance tables are being changed to reflect the tables of the past, which are considered better representations. To compare these modern dancers to other studies of ballet dancers, their ideal weight was recalculated using the same weight tables (Sargent, D. W. (1963). Weight–height relationship of young men and women. *American Journal of Clinical Nutrition, 3*, 199–209).

# 3

# Personal Relationships in the Arts

ook behind any performer and you often see a determined parent who sacrifices time, energy, and money to help the child realize this dream. One assumes that family support is essential to this career, but research indicates that it can be a double-edged sword. Without parents involved in the arts themselves, students are more likely to be in psychotherapy, to have low self-esteem, to doubt themselves, and to fail their training (Butler, 1995; Robson & Gitev, 1991a). Yet I also find problems in supportive households if performers' needs: dominate those of their less or differently talented siblings, become enmeshed with parental needs for achievement, or are bypassed completely by a stage parent (Miller, 1990; Robson & Gitev, 1991b; Tofler et al., 1996). In this chapter, the relationship between the performer's family of origin and his or her personal and professional development are examined.

## THE FAMILY UNIT

Although much has been written about the psychological traits of artists, few researchers have focused on the artist's family background in general or within each of the various art forms. This is surprising, because it is the family that gives us our identity, social status, and economic well-being in all known societies. Ideally, the performer's family will also offer access to the arts, beginning at an early age. My mother tells me that I announced my decision to be a dancer after seeing a televised production of "Sleeping Beauty" by the Royal Ballet—at 2 years old! The memory that I have is going to the ballet around the age of 5 and giving impromptu performances to amused onlookers during each intermission.

Unfortunately, children without such "crystallizing" experiences may not discover their passion for performing or may do so only after it is too late to train. How each family organizes its resources and talents will also affect the mental health of the family members. High levels of parental nurturance are associated with healthy narcissism in offspring, whereas the opposite can lead to a person's inability to establish goals and become too dependent on peers (Buri, Murphy, Richtsmeier, & Komar, 1992).

To understand the family's impact on the performer's development, the literature on families of "gifted children" will be examined. This is an area that traditionally focused on offspring with high IQs, but that has recently come to include other children with special gifts, such as those in math and music (Winner, 1996).

## Families of Gifted Children

In general, families of gifted children combine high expectations for achievement, while providing a supportive and stimulating environment (Winner, 1996). Such parents also are likely to be driven themselves, setting and displaying high standards of excellence. The gifted child contributes to this mix by eliciting positive parental responses that support the desire to learn. There is a dilemma in all this: If their parents are not achievement-oriented, gifted children are less apt to develop to their full potential (Colangelo & Dettman, 1983).

Typically, gifted children occupy a special position within the family hierarchy. In contrast to later-born offspring, they are likely to be the first-born or an only child—an ordinal position that is associated with higher levels of self-esteem on the Narcissistic Personality Inventory (Curtis & Cowell, 1993), which is considered a measure of healthy narcissism (Watson et al., 1995). According to Winner:

> Families focus in two ways on the gifted child's development: either one or both parents spend a great deal of time stimulating and teaching the child themselves, or parents make sacrifices so that the child gets high-level training from the best available teachers. In both cases, family life is totally arranged around the child's needs. Parents channel their interests into their child's talent area and become enormously invested in their child's progress. (Winner, 1996, p. 187)

Winner emphasizes that: "The most extreme cases of child-centered families occur when the child's gift is in a performance domain" (Winner, 1996, p. 188).

The strengths of this situation are obvious, because the parents basically function as allies whose support and sacrifice make it possible for these children to develop an advanced level of expertise. Yet few parents realize the cost this outlay of resources can have on the family, or the consequences of rearing one of their children to be a performer.

Training in the performing arts often begins during childhood, requiring a substantial financial investment and at least one parent's time and energy (Pruett, 1991). A family that is functioning well will adapt, as best as it can, to meet the needs of all its members (Bradshaw, 1988). Yet, even under ideal circumstances, the young performer can monopolize the family's resources, similar to a handicapped or seriously ill child, creating sibling rivalries, interfering with family activities, and burdening the parents' marriage (Berman & McCormick, 1993; Pruett, 1991). Considering the costs, what compels a family to indulge in such a lavish expenditure of its resources?

## The Performer's Lineage

Surveys of art students and performers suggest that a compelling interest in the arts is often passed down from one generation to the next. In a large sample of high school students in Ontario (N=554), parents of arts students were more likely to have a career in the arts than those of gifted or regular students (Robson & Gitev, 1991b). Interestingly, this was not the case for a subgroup of arts students who were under psychiatric care. In addition to having parents with fewer careers in the arts, they were also more likely to come from families marked by separation or divorce. Another study of professional actors and dancers in New York (N=448) inventoried parental interests, as well as their career choices (Reciniello, 1991). While performers' parents were once again found to be involved in the arts, their artistic leanings were greater at the amateur level (fathers = 49%; mothers = 69%) rather than the professional level (fathers = 21%; mothers = 22%).

These results imply that many performers' families are predisposed toward artistic pursuits, even though this bias is not always synonymous with a professional career. This was certainly the case in my family, where my mother was a violinist and my father painted portraits and played the guitar. Does this mean that artistic talent is inherited?

Studies concerning the heritability of talent show that genetic traits, such as musicality, often run in families. Giftedness, on the other hand, appears to be based on "a configuration" of genes (Lykken, McGue, Tellegen, & Bouchard, Jr., 1992). In a study of arts students, the authors assessed the chance of having a musically talented parent and found it to be greater in music students than in those who did not major in this area (Stearns & VanderWoude, 1991). Yet within music itself, the proportion of parents who were gifted singers was no higher for vocal students than for instrumentalists. Thus, although some artistic talent may get passed down to each succeeding generation, giftedness does not.

## The Quality of Parental Investment

Fortunately, even when talent is not shared equally among family members, parents who are involved in the arts as participants or observers can serve as potential helpmates for children who enter a performing arts program. Parents of young performers are often more directive than those of academically gifted children, offering advice, discussing their progress with teachers, and making social comparisons to remind them of the competition. This parental style *is* useful in moderation, because even highly motivated children are less likely to submit to an extensive course of training if left entirely on their own.

In contrast to the talented child who is working with one's parents, those performers who pursue their career against parental wishes often experience a significant decrease in support—a situation that contributes to self-doubt (Nagel, 1988, 1990).

Gender differences are important in generating family assistance. For example, gifted girls often perform better when they do not have brothers who detract from their parents' attention (Winner, 1996). By middle age, creative women who develop or maintain their career ambitions are also those without assertive or talented brothers (Helson, 1990).

Certain art forms also appear to garner parental support for one gender over another. In a national survey conducted at *Dance Magazine* (N=300), young girls cited parental influence as the most common reason for their involvement in dance, unlike male dancers—none of whom began their training at their parents' bidding (Hamilton, 1996). In contrast to Europeans, Americans often view dance as a "feminine" profession, where females are regarded as necessary; girls are in pink tutus, not boys! This negative stereotype may explain why approximately 80% of dance students are female and three times as many women as men become professional dancers in this country (U.S. Census, 1990; Van Dyke, 1996).

Family pressures can also affect whether performers pass or fail their training programs in the arts. In one study (Butler, 1995), failing music students differed from those who passed on several crucial dimensions: their parents were less likely to play music or sing; they experienced more sibling rivalry; and they reported a greater number of family disruptions (e.g., parental separation, divorce, death).

Compared to successful students, those who failed had problems with authority figures and perceived their mothers as anxious and controlling and their fathers as distant or critical. Rather than actively seeking outside help from staff or counselors, these students were more likely to utilize medical services due to poor health. This group also responded to peers as competitors, a fact that may be related to prior sibling rivalry. Finally, failing students were preoccupied with their mother's approval and sibling relationships in contrast to successful students who focused on performing.

In families of performing artists, it would appear that certain changes would be necessary to meet each members' needs. For example, it is conceivable that a support system could be established for siblings to compensate for lack of parental attention, similar to siblings of terminally ill children who occupy center stage. Parental surrogates, such as grandparents, have expressed a desire to play a more active (and satisfying) role in rearing their grandchildren. Financial aid may also be crucial in the family's overall adjustment, especially in the case of single-parent households. Lastly, a greater emphasis on the arts in education would benefit children whose families lack a background in this area.

A lack of parental investment in the arts, family pressures, and sibling rivalry all create a toll on the young performer's ability to function in this profession. Thus, a nurturing environment would appear to be a crucial aspect of training to be a performer. This influence should be distinguished, however, from involvement that masquerades as support, when the parent's narcissistic needs come to dominate those of the gifted child's. In the latter case, a stage parent is born.

## THE STAGE PARENT

To some extent, a stage parent is similar to all parents who strongly identify with their children and want them to do well. The difference is that this identification is taken to an extreme, because the parent's self-worth depends on the fruition of the child's talent. A recent term coined to describe this parent–child relationship in gymnastics is "achievement by proxy" (Tofler et al., 1996). Likened to a form of child abuse, its hallmark is strong parental encouragement of a potentially dangerous endeavor with the goal of achieving fame and fortune through a child.

Gymnastics, with its high incidence of injuries, stunted development, and eating disorders, offers a graphic display of what happens to children who are pushed beyond their natural limitations. However, even when there is no danger of physical injury, parents who exploit their children's talent to meet their own needs for success can be hurtful as well. In a sample of intellectually gifted children, offspring identified by their parents' nomination in the British National Association for Gifted Children were less personally and socially adjusted than intellectually gifted children whose parents had not joined this organization (Freeman, 1979). Both teachers and parents described these children as difficult, emotional and overly sensitive, with sleep problems and no friends.

### Characteristic Behavior of Stage Parents

Above all else, stage parents want their children to outperform others. In pursuit of this goal, they often set sky-high goals that are vaguely defined and continually out of reach. During competitions, it is common for superachieving parents to issue numerous instructions, overreact to minor mistakes or failures, and get into power struggles with teachers (Shelov & Kelly, 1991). Typically, these parents' communications revolve around their perceptions of the child's needs and dreams, making them dominating and intrusive. Although this parental style can be helpful during times of crisis, the constant pressure that is placed on the child to excel can cause serious harm.

Another characteristic behavior of certain stage parents is to bend over backward to accommodate their child's schedule, while making them exempt from family chores like cleaning their rooms. Instead, a gruelling routine of classes, rehearsals and performances may fill their child's waking hours. This is a potential trap because these children often grow into adults who are ill-prepared to take responsibility for their own lives, whether it is paying taxes, voting, or taking another person's feelings into account.

## The Downside of Competition

Is the child's performance ever good enough? If you listen to a stage parent, you notice that success is constantly being redefined. If the child becomes top in her music class, then this parent changes the goal to becoming top in the entire school. If another child takes private classes in addition to a full schedule, then the talented boy should double his load. Or are these parents' goals simply open-ended, being molded to whatever the child has not yet accomplished? Under these circumstances, I see noncompetitive children withdraw, whereas those with a high need to achieve may work harder, albeit with mounting insecurities and resentments.

How parents handle defeat will also be important to these children because, similar to sports, failure in the performing arts occurs in public with others watching. In sports, negative evaluations from parents (as well as coaches and peers) add to the young athlete's anxiety, with habitual criticism leading to stage fright (Brustad, 1988; Smith & Smoll, 1990). I often see a backlash when young performers finally escape this excessive parental pressure; they stop achieving because they are no longer compelled to perform without their parents' nagging.

A serious consequence of stress due to competition in children is dropping out (Gould, Feltz, & Weiss, 1985; Klint & Weiss, 1986). Others may include depression, illness or injury. In my study of ballet students at the School of American Ballet (N=40), 55% had stopped dance training at this exclusive school over a four-year-period (Hamilton et al., in press). Besides anatomical problems that made it more difficult to dance, these young performers had more injuries, eating disorders, and negative feelings about their bodies. The following case highlights the anguish that performers feel when parents push them to compete regardless of the personal cost.

### Case 3.0
### The Captive Singer

A 24-year-old female singer in musical theater came to see me for depression, after a series of unsuccessful auditions. Although it had only been three months since her last job in summer stock, she had become increasingly anxious, tearful, and hopeless with each rejection, eventually withdrawing from her friends and avoiding opportunities to try out for new roles. I learned that this performer had suffered for years because of her parents' drive for success and harsh disciplinary actions whenever she retreated from competition. In response to their negative sanctions, this singer would become depressed, and had made one half-hearted attempt at suicide with aspirin in her teens. Another defining moment occurred as an adult, when she became engaged to a man overseas. Again, her parents saw this move as a threat to her career, and she was pushed into terminating the relationship. At the time that I saw her, this young woman was desperate to make a career transition but felt paralyzed by parental pressures to remain a performer.

## How Common are Stage Parents?

Although no one really knows just how prevalent stage parents are in the performing arts, family problems seem to be the rule rather than the exception. In a study of celebrated figures in the 20th century, 70% of the artists had difficult family lives compared to 56% of scientists (Goertzel, Goertzel & Goertzel, 1978). Because of my own interest in this subject, I carried out a small survey on professional performers (N=30) and found that 14% had one or both parents who were excessively involved in this career. One of my taped interviews was with a leading performer who continued to feel burdened by his father's expectations years later. Tragically, I learned that he went on to commit suicide six months after our interview. His words hint at the turmoil inside.

> My relationship with my father was very difficult. Very strict. Very severe. Very demanding in terms of performance in school, in the arts, in emotional conduct, in everything. There wasn't any way that I could relax. One thing I've never mentioned that just pops into my mind is resentment. I must have resented the extremity of his demands but I never admitted it to myself. Now, I find that I'm just as hard on myself. It's strange because I'm also feeling like it's more and more difficult to feel a good, healthy sense of my own motivation. My own satisfaction in performing. I know it's because I never...the fact that I was never able to say "Come on dad, it's enough, lay off! It's too much."

## The Consequences of Being a "Star"

Children with stage parents, like the late 6-year-old beauty pageant winner, Jon-Benet Ramsey, may struggle with a worldview where their sole value lies in what they can accomplish. In *The Drama of the Gifted Child* (1990), Alice Miller describes case studies of children with emotionally disabled parents who owned and exploited their offsprings' talent. These cases illustrate how, rather than focusing on the child's needs, hopes, and dreams, it is the parent's needs that become the prime motivation for achievement. The outcome is insidious. The child's talent becomes a mechanism to guarantee a secure parental relationship, but ownership of this talent is thrown into contention, thwarting normal growth and development.

Sadly, children with narcissistically involved parents often have an overwhelming need for external validation, making them "professional" achievers who constantly push themselves to excel (Donaldson-Pressman & Pressman, 1994). Unfortunately, the emotional price can be costly, because current perceptions of one's family of origin account for about 13% of the variance in self-esteem, self-efficacy and depression (Oliver & Paull, 1995).

In the above study, the adult offspring who exhibit problems in these areas report a parental rearing style characterized by "affectionless control." Besides producing a negative family climate, these parental behaviors signify a lack of acceptance regarding one's children who must be controlled by negative psychological techniques, such as guilt-induction and criticism. In contrast to authoritive parents where there is a clear set of moral standards, "authoritarian" parents are rigid and dictatorial (Winner, 1996). Not surprisingly, these socialization patterns are associated with low self-esteem, even when offsprings' current mood is controlled statistically. Rebellion and disaffection may also result.

No matter how talented they are, children need to feel worthy of attention apart from their productivity; yet this often means that parents walk a tightrope between being involved realistically in a child's career and being intrusive, because both factors are important. Stage parents also must maintain realistic expectations about their "star," while meeting their own achievement needs and not relying solely on their children.

## PEER REVIEW

The gifted child's family life has a substantial effect on how he or she interacts with others in the performing arts community. Children whose parents actively encourage them to outshine others often have trouble relinquishing this competitive mindset, putting them in continual opposition to their peers. Parents who insist on extra classes with little down time for play in adolescence also make it difficult for young performers to "fit in" and be in tune with the dominant culture. This conflict between the need to achieve and being "one of the crowd" is not easy to resolve, often leading to low self-esteem in those who feel the most different from their peers.

### Personal Isolation

Unfortunately, even under the best of circumstances, the all-encompassing nature of training leaves students with few outside sources of support. An epidemiological study of 375 arts students from Ontario showed that they had significantly fewer friendships compared to regular academic students (Robson & Gitev, 1991a). Instead of hanging out after school with their peers, 74% of music students and 60% of drama students took additional classes or courses in their art form. This was in stark contrast to regular academic students, where 55% reported free time.

Being "out of sync" with classmates has both social and emotional consequences. Estimates suggest that roughly one out of every four intellectually gifted children has problems in these areas versus half this number in regular school children (Janos & Robinson, 1985). Many of us believe that by labeling these children "gifted" and accelerating them in school, we cause them to feel different from their peers (like a misfit), which then becomes a component of their self-concept. This is related to poorer adjustment and lower self-esteem, even when these children feel superior, compared to those not identified as gifted (Janos, Fung, & Robinson, 1985; Kaplan, 1983).

In contrast, performers are rarely labeled because of their talent or segregated from their agemates in school; yet they often feel special because of their achievements. In one study, arts students had a better self-concept in their relationships with same-sexed peers than either gifted or regular high school students (Robson & Gitev, 1991b). Most of these students also viewed their friends as supportive rather than competitive. Research shows the same healthy picture in a group of teenage girls in ballet whose psychosocial adjustment was similar to the norm except for one important dimension—their sexual functioning was impaired (Hamilton et al., 1997). This finding may be due to the athletic aspects of dance, which affect physical development. The greater the delay in puberty (i.e., breast and pubic stage), the more these dancers expressed uncertainty toward the opposite sex. The next step is to examine peer relationships among others types of performers.

## Competition versus Cooperation

To do their best in the performing arts, children must combine above-average ability with a burning desire to achieve their goals. Wise parents who make a point of setting goals that are finite and concrete (e.g., getting to practice on time) give their enterprising child an opportunity to build self-esteem in contrast to open-ended goals, where success is always out of reach.

Research shows that people care more about where their performance stands within a group than the group's overall success—an effect that is strongest among those with lower collective self-esteem (McFarland & Buehler, 1995). Thus, difficulties emerge for performers who become hypercompetitive. In the previous study of arts students (Robson & Gitev, 1991b), the advantages that this group had in their personal relationships diminished for those in psychotherapy, where two-thirds felt competitive with their peers. It should come as no surprise that these students also had fewer friends.

## The Benefits of Friendship

Admittedly, although it is never easy for a performer to keep company with someone who is competing for the same roles, isolation can be a problem because social support helps to reduce stress (Rook, 1987). Friendships take these benefits one step further by increasing the levels of intimacy, mutuality, and reciprocity. Friends also share their feelings because they enjoy doing so, not just to enhance their coping skills.

Does having a friend help us at work? When we look at research on achievement, we find that several aspects of friendship mediate the experience of burnout (Kruger, Bernstein, & Botman, 1995). In this study, friendship among team members in a work environment is related to a greater sense of accomplishment and lower levels of emotional exhaustion. Discussing work-related concerns with friends also reduces depersonalization. Yet the most influential aspect of these friendships is "having fun" together which, the authors speculate, may help people approach a task with renewed vigor. The conclusion? Successful groups strike a balance between task performance and members' emotional and social needs.

Being socially at ease with one's peers is more difficult in certain art forms, such as music, where six hours a day may be spent in solitary practice. Still, sacrifices are necessary for all performers.

I gave up the Brownies, dating, and college to pursue my dream of dancing in the New York City Ballet. Teenagers who have a great need to "fit in" with their peers may find this choice increasingly difficult to make. A broad set of social interests can also sway you from your goal, causing gifted children to drop out over time (Tomlinson-Keasey & Little, 1990). The opposite scenario, which involves narrowing your focus to one target, helps performers excel but carries with it a number of interpersonal stresses.

### Classical Dance and Music

The "team" spirit shared by members in a performing art can be extremely rewarding; however, each art form continues to exert its own unique constraints. Ballet, for instance, is considered by many to be a "feminine" profession that focuses on the ballerina, while limiting the male to only occasional moments of technical display. Besides influencing many parents' decision to support their daughters in dance, the relationship between the sexes may also be fraught with tension.

Research on masculine gender-role stress suggests that men experience higher levels of anger and anxiety and engage in poorer health habits if they are outperformed at work by females (Eisler, Skidmore, & Ward, 1988). Research on leading dancers and musicians in New York City showed that the male dancers were significantly less enterprising and adjusted and more depressed than the average male, while the women reported fewer mood fluctuations and were genuinely fulfilled from their work (Hamilton et al., 1995). These findings suggest that ballet may favor female dancers who occupy center stage.

This was not the case in the music profession, as both males and females differed markedly from the norm. Unlike the opposing gender roles in dance, the roles of musicians in modern orchestras, chamber ensembles, or solo performances are usually not differentiated by sex.

The past-president of the American Federation of Musicians, Local 802, has attributed this bias to World War II, when women filled the ranks of absent men (J. Glasel, personal communication, October 1992). The result is that auditions are now conducted sight unseen, subjecting all musicians to an enforced equality. Although this has helped female performers to get past the longstanding bias against them in music, interpersonal stress is a universal complaint.

Because professional musicians engage in extended freelance work, both sexes are forced to adapt to each other as well as to unique work expectations and demands. On an interpersonal level, this apparent parity can translate into constant vying between men and women for a say on small artistic decisions. In the present sample, both sexes were significantly more hostile and less caring and adaptive than the norm. Yet only the men were significantly less adjusted and more withdrawn, whereas female musicians were remarkably more independent, sociable, and fulfilled from their work. A musical career may force women to become more autonomous to counteract the subtle forms of discrimination, whereas men may become uncomfortable with the enforced equality and withdraw.

## Love Relationships

Besides relating to colleagues, personal development means separating from your family of origin and forming an intimate adult relationship with another person. This goal can be challenging due to the insular lifestyle of many performers in this community, as well as differing expectations both inside and outside the profession.

The nature of theatrical life, with its intense focus on the self, can make performers challenging mates, particularly for people outside show business. During a Broadway season or the making of a film, it is not unusual for many performers to become completely absorbed in their work. A lover may interpret this behavior as a sign of withdrawal or disinterest in the relationship. At times, the performer's need to be idolized on stage may also be carried home in the way of childish demands for attention, especially if there is a deeply rooted emotional insecurity. Rumor has it that Rita Hayworth, describing life with Orson Wells, said that when he awoke each morning he expected her to applaud. I find that partners who are "in love" with the performer's aura of glamour on stage also can become easily disillusioned when hidden insecurities and worries are exposed.

Performers may be tempted to stray from their primary relationship into a series of short-term affairs, because the close proximity between colleagues in a show or film often leads to a heightened sense of intimacy. You might think that if two performers were to become involved, the relationship would go more smoothly, right? Wrong! Competition all too often gets in the way as one person's career takes off or the other takes a downward slide, making them out of sync.

Last, but not least, the amount of energy that it takes to excel in the performing arts leaves little time to raise a family. Among professionals who become eminent, women are more likely to remain single compared to men, and less likely to have children if they marry at all (Winner, 1996).

## TRANSFERENCE AND THE ROLE OF THE LEADER

Throughout this book, I have shown how performing depends, at first, on one's training with influential teachers, and later on the close direction of directors and choreographers. Like all forms of supervision, these roles involve the exertion of authority, which can elicit strong reactions by tapping into people's experiences with their family of origin (Lowman, 1993).

Conflicts at work often emerge in settings that reawaken unresolved issues from performers' pasts, as they project their hopes, desires, fears, and needs onto authority figures, as well as the work setting in general. In their mind's eye, directors assume the role of parents, colleagues become siblings, and senior administrators are even treated as grandparents.

Depending on their family history, performers may view these figures as allies, benevolent gods, or tyrants. Remember, many professionals grow up in an atmosphere where they had to "perform" for their parents' approval, whereas others used overwork as the primary means of escaping from a difficult homelife. These family dynamics contribute to patterns of overcommitment connected to burnout (Lowman, 1993). The parental bond also influences the way performers relate to teachers, directors, and choreographers. People who possess negative feelings about their upbringing often have trouble trusting others.

How much does one's family of origin affect the quality of professional relationships? It seems that the family dynamics of dancers in a ballet company affect the relationship they have with the artistic director (Hamilton et al., 1991).

Our study confirmed that dancers feel intensely about their director in the New York City Ballet, where George Balanchine occupied this position for 35 years. Eighty-six percent of the dancers idealized this director as a powerful father figure in their lives. They also manifested strong feelings toward the company at large, with 59% describing their membership in relational terms that focused on family and a sense of security.

Were the dancers's relationships with Balanchine based on transference—that is to say, reenactments from the past? The dancers were asked to consider their role in how they got along with this director. Surprisingly, only a few believed that their determination (10%) and talent (7%) were important, while 83% felt that a personal vulnerability, such as anxiety, dependency, or a need to please him contributed to the dynamics of the interaction. The dancers' family of origin was then explored in order to gain some insight into the underlying themes.

First, the similarities between the parental and professional bonds on several relevant dimensions were examined. For example, transference occurred if the performer experienced conflict around the need to separate in both of these relationships. The results showed that many dancers responded to Balanchine with feelings, attitudes or behaviors that repeated their early parent–child relationships. Sixty-two percent replayed patterns that were consistent with their fathers; a 14% similarity rate existed with the maternal relationship, and 17% reacted in ways previously exhibited with both parents.

Next, three specific characteristics of the parental attachment (i.e., was it close, distant, or dominating?) and the way their professional relationship changed over time were examined. Dancers whose mothers were emotionally unavailable (14%) during their childhood grew increasingly distant from Balanchine over the years, while feeling close with their mothers (76%) led to a better relationship with this director.

What about the father? It turns out that having an authoritarian father (21%) affected their ties with this director as well, marking it by fear and retreat throughout the course of their careers. Yet unlike the maternal relationship, proximity with the father was not as crucial. Instead, dancers who were distant from their fathers (48%) were less likely to focus on Balanchine's human qualities, whereas those who were close (52%) had a positive response to his criticisms.

What we are seeing here is that the family of origin can have a significant impact on performers' professional ties in the arts. In this study, close to two-thirds of these performers repeated patterns previously experienced with their fathers in response to Balanchine's absolute authority, and even more dancers put him up on a pedestal. As mentioned earlier, self psychologists see idealization as having an important role in consolidating developmentally crucial interpersonal relationships.

According to Kohut (1977), the child seeks two fundamental types of relationships with early caretakers that express basic narcissistic needs. The need to form an idealized image of at least one parent is generally directed toward the father, who represents the ideals and values to which the individual strives. In contrast, the mother's role provides a sense of grandiosity, or feeling special, by mirroring the infant's evolving capacities.

This mirroring pattern was not a prevalent theme in our sample; even when the director praised his dancers, only one-third experienced this praise as reflecting their ability in dance. Balanchine's role in this company most likely commanded a stereotypical father response. In addition, because Kohut believes that the need for narcissistic gratification continues throughout the person's lifetime, idealization of an omnipotent and all-perfect other remains an important avenue of pursuit.

Interestingly, the mother's influence was evident in the quality of this relationship over time. Dancers with distant mothers grew apart from Balanchine, whereas those who were close became more intimate with him throughout the course of their careers. Bowlby (1973) suggests that the attachment to the mother, who is usually the primary caretaker, forms the basis of interpersonal trust in later life. This relationship differs from that with the father, who is often less involved in childrearing. In the latter case, the attachment in infancy develops more slowly and appears to be less intense. In this group, only fear exhibited in their paternal relationship was found to influence the proximity with the director. Thus, Balanchine also may have represented a primary attachment figure to these dancers, as the degree of intimacy with their mothers was re-enacted with this director over time.

## Interventions

When I see performers who exhibit conflicts with authority, my immediate response is to determine the reality of the complaint, as well as how amenable the work setting and the individual are to change. Whereas film directors are known to use psychological consultants to resolve conflicts at work, most performing arts organizations do not welcome such scrutiny. In most cases, the options available to the troubled performer include learning how to adjust and work with a difficult supervisor, or finding another job.

In the next chapter, I will examine another hazard in this profession due to performance anxiety. Although a certain amount of anxiety is a normal reaction to performing in front of others, stage fright can be an excruciating problem that may easily derail a career.

# 4

# Focusing the Spotlight on Performance

A
nyone who steps before the footlights knows that performing on stage can be exhilarating—or terrifying. Yet the audience sees only the artist's persona, not the fears that lie beneath the mask. Beginning with their first audition at an arts academy, performers learn to deny vulnerability in the presence of others, whether it is the threat of rejection or the failure to live up to their own potential. Still, the fear of being evaluated remains ubiquitous.

In the general population, performance anxiety is the third most common mental problem, exceeded only by alcoholism and depression (Azar, 1995). This disorder is even more common in performing artists, who often attempt to combat the symptoms associated with the "fight-or-flight" syndrome with alcohol and drugs (Clark & Agras, 1991; Hamilton & Kella, 1992; Lehrer, 1987). This chapter examines the various components of stage fright that affect the person's cognitive, physical, and behavioral functioning. For performers, it can be a debilitating disorder that places their self-esteem on the line in every production.

## THE QUEST FOR APPROVAL

As a former dancer, I know from personal experience that few things are more devastating than not being cast for a favorite role. Yet this wish to perform on stage before an audience also carries with it a significant price when it is granted; namely, how do you separate your self-worth from the evaluations of others?

Whether it is a theater, movie house, or MTV, performers who display their talent before others are exposed and vulnerable. A scathing review in *The New York Times* or *Billboard* magazine will affect their prospects now, as well as their future in the entertainment industry. Although some artists cope with this uncertainty, others find that their self-esteem fluctuates dramatically, depending on their approval rating for the moment. The fear of being publicly humiliated is a strong component of performance anxiety, leading to self-doubt and a constant need for approval (Pezenick, 1992).

### Performing on Stage: The Reality

Unlike law or medicine, there is no clear-cut way to move ahead in the performing arts no matter how talented you may be. A lawyer who produces for a firm over two decades can hope, even in today's uncertain job market, to become a partner fully vested in the pension plan with at least the grudging respect of the junior members. Work opportunities as a performer arise seemingly by magic.

Apart from the subjective appraisal of the performer's talent, an important role may appear because of his or her age, "look," ethnicity, vocal range, luck, or all of the above. Unfortunately, audition personnel rarely give feedback, so it is easy for performers to take rejection personally, particularly if they are desperate to find work. According to the latest census (1990), the average salary of the two-thirds of performing artists who are employed on a part-time basis is $18,098 annually.

Sadly, these tenuous work conditions do not change even with full-time employment. Orchestral musicians and opera singers must reaudition at regular intervals to keep their positions as members of a company, and the maximum time a union contract will guarantee work for a member of a dance company is one year. Recently, I questioned a union representative from the American Guild of Musical Artists about the short length of dance contracts only to be told that "dancers do not get tenure." No wonder performers are insecure!

Celebrity status brings more money and, hopefully, more options; however, there is still no such thing as long-term job security in the performing arts. Instead, big stars still have to compete for roles, while a constant influx of younger talent seeks to take their place. This fact was brought home to me in my clinical practice not too long ago when an Oscar-winning actor came to see me in tears. She was middle-aged, no longer able to support herself through acting, and had developed a full-blown case of stage fright on the rare occasions when she performed a role. We finally decided that she might regain some sense of security by going back to acting class.

The entertainment industry's bias toward youth, rather than experience, is a particular problem in film and dance, where aging can even undermine the popular appeal of a child star, such as Shirley Temple. Some progress is being made on this front now that women no longer wear the heavy makeup and severe hairstyles that made them look older in the past before the more youthful 1960s. However, we still have a long way to go. Just read *The Guinness Book of Movie Facts & Feats* on all 1990 movie releases in the United States and see that only two out of five of today's leading ladies are over the age of 40 (Robertson, 1994).

Having started my own performing career at the ripe age of 16, I can tell you that being young and physically fit is even more important in dance. If we look at the roster published in the same year of 1990 for the New York City Ballet where I performed, we see that 3% of the dancers are over 40, all are male, and most do character roles. In 1997, one female dancer, Merrill Ashley, falls into this category; a fact considered to be so unusual that she was featured on CNN. In fact, most ballet dancers have to retire in their early 30s, because of injuries or the ever-changing whims of their artistic director.

Because of the real insecurity that permeates this profession, the pressure to produce at a high level is constant for all performers, whether they are one of the young and talented or an aging Pavarotti trying to nail a high C for an audience that would just as soon "Boo" as yell "Bravo." The safest bet would appear to aim at being flawless; however, the fact remains that "practice does not make perfect."

Every performer is subject to bad reviews, an unresponsive audience, or an off day because of overwork or illness. Physical decline is also a factor, requiring various adjustments over time. Performers who deny these realities tend to be their own worst critics, dissecting their work into "good and bad" components with no appreciation for subtle lapses in neuromuscular and mental control (Plaut, 1988; Srivastava, 1989; Wolfe, 1989). This practice leads to a number of myths and cognitive distortions, some of which have a negative impact on performance.

## Common Myths and Distortions

Many performers share a common myth that seasoned veterans should always find performing easy, and being anxious about this work is seen as a sign of trouble or weakness. In reality, performing is tough, requiring a set of complex skills that may be more difficult to pull off in certain situations (e.g., live theater versus film). Anxiety about performing is also a universal phenomenon and may actually be necessary to keep a performance from being "flat" (Azar, 1995). Of course, the emotional manifestations of anxiety may have a positive impact (e.g., arousal and intensity) or negative impact (e.g., apprehension and distractibility), depending on the individual's response (Wolfe, 1989).

Misinformation about a person's talent also adds fuel to the fire in talented performers who believe that they will never be "good enough," no matter how hard they try. If you recall, gifted students who excel in performance settings function according to an "incremental theory," which is based on the belief that one improves by seeking out new challenges and learning from past mistakes (Dweck, 1995). In contrast, performers who operate according to an "entity theory" view their talent as having a fixed amount, making them fearful of any test that could reveal that their special gift is flawed.

In my work with performers, I find that common cognitive distortions often accentuate the negative aspects of performance (Burns, 1980; Steptoe & Fidler, 1987). For example, a common distortion in performers involves "all-or-nothing" thinking, where they interpret even small imperfections as a sign of failure. Other self-defeating patterns include assuming the worst from ambiguous feedback, exaggerating the impact of problems in their lives, and downplaying personal assets that could be sources of self-esteem. Emotional reasoning, where negative feelings about themselves are elevated to the status of truth, also miss the target and may foster panic about performing.

## Anxiety in Performers

The primary characteristic of performance anxiety is the fear of doing something that could lead to a humiliating or embarrassing moment in front of others. However, the extent to which stage fright dominates performers' lives can vary widely, ranging from a mild, transient, and well-concealed sense of discomfort during the first few minutes of walking on to the stage to feelings of stark terror accompanied by a panic attack (Plaut, 1988).

In pronounced cases, some of the symptoms, such as deafening palpitations, losing control of one's expressive functions, and depersonalization may be more disabling than others. A dry mouth appears to be the most troublesome problem to wind players, whereas string players often become distressed over cold hands, sweaty palms, lack of finger dexterity, and a sense of panic (Wolfe, 1989).

Generally, stage fright is disabling when the degree of terror feels unbearable or the performer is no longer able to mask it. Musicians and singers are particularly prone to the negative aspects of anxiety because when they perform a note off-key or out of sequence it may be obvious to even the most unsophisticated ear. Dancers and actors have a bit more leeway to cover their mistakes. Although, if it is the third act of *Swan Lake*, most of the regulars in the audience will know if the ballerina fails to complete her thirty-two fouettes (i.e., whipping turns on one leg). The actor with stage fright may forget his lines, and the comic may be unable to improvise to the hecklers in the crowd.

Importantly, when performers are unable to live up to their own high expectations, the discrepancy between reality and their personal aspirations can be especially painful.

## DISCREPANCIES BETWEEN THE REAL AND IDEAL SELF

Most people in the performing arts are preoccupied with self-actualization, holding on to a vision of who they want to become over time. When they succeed at being their best, the discrepancy between their real and ideal self-evaluations is reduced, leading to greater personal adjustment (Hamilton, 1988a).

Although people often see themselves as better than they really are, it is often mediated by individual differences in narcissism (Taylor & Brown, 1988). People who are low on normal narcissism are more likely to judge their own performance as inadequate, even when their abilities are sufficient for the task at hand (John & Robins, 1994). Experiencing defects in the ideal self is a painful reaction that strikes at the heart of the person's identity and can lead to shame (Morrison, 1986).

Within the psychoanalytic literature, some theorists view shame as a "superficial" response that is connected to external expectations embedded in the social network (Lowenfield, 1976). Morrison (1986), however, believes that shame occurs when a person feels *incapable* of living up to his or her own cherished ideals in relation to a "perceiving other." Viewed from a self-psychological perspective, this would be a repugnant experience that is far from superficial. Thus, in contrast to guilt, which follows some omission or commission of regretted behavior, shame occurs when the person sees the self as impotent. The question is, who is most vulnerable to this narcissistic insult?

Examination of Kohut's (1977) theory on narcissistic development finds that the child initially needs a "mirroring" parental figure who can reflect the self's evolving capacities, followed by an idealized image of at least one parent that permits fusion with an all-perfect other. Under optimal conditions, these relationships form the "bipolar" self, which is a permanent psychic structure based on healthy ambitions and strongly held ideals and values.

The sense of feeling special originates in the mother's eye, and it has a lot to do with how a person feels about himself or herself. Consequently, if this aspect of the bipolar self is flawed (i.e., the exhibitionistic self), Morrison believes that we need to compensate through the second pole of narcissistic development, which involves the pursuit of ideals. So even though this pole substitutes for the defective or missing self-regulating structure, it also leaves the person prone to shame when this too meets with failure. Not surprisingly, narcissism plays a significant role in the stage-fright phenomenon (Gabbard, 1983).

## Early Signs of Distress

I have noticed that many performers with stage fright report an early history of being hypersensitive to criticism or rejection from others. Often, they had difficulty asserting themselves in appropriate situations and felt stymied by low self-esteem and feelings of inferiority. This scenario led, in many cases, to underachievement at a performing arts school or on the job, as anxiety kept them from competing with colleagues and interacting with figures of authority.

Typically, these performers' anxiety also permeated their social world, which resulted in a decreased access to social support. By the time I see them, they may be isolated from others or clinging to unfulfilling relationships. At times, they are still living at home as adults.

Another early sign of distress for professionals and students includes having anxiety before a special event. It may be weeks before the affair, yet the performer is completely obsessed with the possibility of making humiliating mistakes, worried about being too ill to perform, or has imagined the negative comments of critics and the audience. As the stakes rise, so can the level of anxiety, often leading performers to make radical changes in their work habits (Clark, 1989). It is around this time that they may take three classes a day or practice a musical selection until exhaustion, only later realizing that such precipitous changes in practice lead to overuse phenomena (e.g., carpal tunnel syndrome in musicians; ankle tendonitis in dancers; vocal chord polyps in singers).

Anxiety also can narrow a person's attention; it tends to keep the performer's concentration focused on the self rather than the task at hand. A well-rehearsed piece that is usually played automatically now becomes the subject of intense scrutiny, often getting in the way of other artistic aspects of performance, such as style, interpretation, and communication with the audience.

Needless to say, this response detracts from the overall performance and may lead to increasing errors, including losing one's place. This is when a performer may feel conflicted about investing himself or herself in the artistic process, due to the potential loss of self-esteem. In one study of 94 musicians with stage fright, 30% of these performers had stopped performing or left the profession because of this debilitating problem (Clark & Agras, 1991).

The combination of fear of failure, the expectation of social disapproval, loss of composure, and the possibility of panicking on stage can make performing an excruciating experience. An example of how difficult this experience can be is seen in the words of the late Sir Lawrence Olivier (1982), who admitted to having suffered from severe stage fright for five years unbeknownst to his audience. He remembered his reaction of dread in his autobiography:

> With each succeeding minute it became less possible to resist this terror. My cue came, and on I went to that stage where I knew with grim certainty I would not be capable of remaining more than a few minutes. I began to watch for the instant at which my knowledge of my next line would vanish. Only the next two, now, no—one more...I started to fade, my throat closed up and the audience was beginning to go giddily round. (Olivier, 1982, p. 261)

## Coping with the Stress of Performing

The fear of stepping on to the stage leads to a number of rituals and superstitions that are passed down through each succeeding generation. For example, I found out early in ballet that it is considered to be good luck if a dancer pricks her finger and bleeds on her toe shoe before a performance. Feeble as it sounds, it did give me a momentary sense of security.

Later, I learned through my clinical practice that an actor who gets a "call back" for a part wears the same outfit he used for the first audition—it might jinx him to change clothing. All performers also believe that you should never tempt fate by wishing someone good luck before an event. Instead, dancers who want to support their colleagues say "merde" (i.e., shit), actors say "break a leg," opera singers say "in boco lupo" (i.e., in the mouth of the wolf), and comedians say nothing at all. One comic I was seeing said that their group is just too competitive to offer any words of wisdom or support.

What do performers do when performance anxiety occurs? The research shows that all too many professionals attempt to control their symptoms through self-medication.

In the large survey of musicians diagnosed with stage fright, 97% said that their performance was impaired because of anxiety (Clark & Agras, 1991). Of this group, 41% had used alcohol as a method of reducing their anxiety whereas only 24% sought out psychotherapy. I believe that performers often shy away from therapy because they are trained from an early age to deny feelings of anxiety. Many performers also find out through word-of-mouth that beta-blockers can reduce the physiological signs of stress. In the present study, more full-time professionals (67%) used these medications than part-time professionals (37%), students (13%), serious amateurs (13%), or casual amateurs (00%).

The use of beta-blockers (FDA approved for the treatment of heart problems and hypertension) inhibits peripheral sympathetic arousal, making it particularly attractive to musicians to combat somatic symptoms, such as tremors. As a result, performers often pass around these medications illicitly to maintain their competitive edge, similar to steroid use in athletes. In the survey of professional musicians previously cited, 26% used these medications for performance anxiety. Over two-thirds of musicians (70%) do not have medical supervision for these prescription drugs (Fishbein, Middlestadt, Ottati, Straus, & Ellis, 1988).

Research on a group of professional violinists and violists (N=34) who had performed an average of 13 years within the competitive arena of New York showed that 45% used beta-blockers to reduce stage fright, obtaining most of these drugs from colleagues and family members (Hamilton & Kella, 1992). This is a serious problem, because side effects include weight gain, nightmares, muscle fatigue and, in some cases, depression (Lehrer, Rosen, Kostis, & Greenfield, 1987). Beta-blockers are also contraindicated in certain cases, such as congestive heart failure and bronchial asthma, and may mask the signs of hypoglycemia.

Few performers with stage fright know about these problems or the potential for substance abuse when they rely on alcohol and prescription drugs (Raeburn, 1987). Unfortunately, no substance is totally harmless and addiction (psychological and/or physical) is a real possibility. For this reason, the choice to self-medicate for performance anxiety is often similar to playing Russian roulette. Some people use drugs and alcohol occasionally without harmful consequences; others get hooked or worse.

Performers may use psychoactive drugs to put themselves in a more relaxed state of mind. Nevertheless, they should not ignore the possible long-term problems and dangers, such as impaired performance, drug tolerance and physical dependence. If the drug is discontinued, withdrawal symptoms can also lead to nausea, anxiety, severe stomach cramps, delirium, convulsions, and sometimes even death. Finally, all drugs can cause a psychological dependence, so that the effects are deemed necessary to maintain a sense of well-being.

A different problem occurs when performers use illegal drugs; they cannot control the ingredients whether these are toxic chemicals in cocaine or high levels of THC (a synthetic derivative of marijuana). Today, the purity in heroin on the street can skyrocket from 60% to a staggering 90%, sending unknowing recipients to the hospital. Aside from the possible misdemeanor charge for using drugs or felony charge for possessing larger amounts, which suggests an intent to sell, the unpredictable nature of illegal drugs vastly increases the health risk every time they are used. Furthermore, if more than one drug is taken at a time, the resulting drug interaction can be fatal.

## The Nature of Resiliency

What are the alternatives to self-medication? Although there is no simple remedy for performance anxiety, certain practices can help. First, a reliable support system can bolster people during times of stress, while restoring their self-esteem by confirming their valuable traits (Taylor & Brown, 1988). Other assets that help with stress include activities that provide additional creative outlets for self-expression, as well as financial support. Along these lines, Harrison Ford, the actor, managed to survive many bleak years in Hollywood before he achieved success by working as a carpenter—a role that he said curbed his desperation by rewarding him spiritually and financially.

Under duress, performers' mental activities can also repair, restore, or otherwise stabilize their psychological equilibrium. For example, individuals with high self-esteem go a long way to maintain this state by viewing negative feedback as less credible than positive feedback, and interpreting ambiguous information in a way that is more favorable than reality. Many resilient performers use these strategies in the face of criticism, as well as in auditions where feedback is often lacking.

People with low self-esteem, in contrast, may cling to the ideals of their profession and feel a significant depletion of the self when criticized. If some performers have a large discrepancy between their real self and their "the way it should be" self, then they may have a harder time bouncing back from disappointments. The self-esteem of performers who constantly compare themselves to others is also vulnerable, because it is easy for someone else's gain to become a symbol of their loss. Self-defeating behaviors that impair resiliency may require professional help.

## THE ETIOLOGY OF PERFORMANCE ANXIETY

Stage fright is not limited to performers—it exists in people in all types of performance settings, such as pilots, public speakers, students taking exams, and athletes. Anxiety under these circumstances is normal. However, the American Psychiatric Association recommends that we give a diagnosis of Social Phobia if the degree of distress and disruption involves a pathological reaction to performance (APA, 1994).

Although no one really knows the cause of social phobia, it is considered a variant of the fight-or-flight syndrome described by Cannon (1929). Symptoms tend to emerge in the mid-teens, with a lifetime prevalence rate that ranges from 3% to 13%. Importantly, this disorder appears to run in families where the relative risk is more than three times higher than in normal controls (Fyer, Mannuzza, Chapman, Liebowitz, & Klein, 1993). People with a diagnosis of social phobia have double the risk of becoming depressed and dependent on alcohol (Azar, 1995). Relatives also have a higher risk of major depressive disorder, although twin studies are needed to separate genetic from environmental influences.

It is also important to differentiate between: a) "state" anxiety, which is transient and situation-specific, and b) "trait" anxiety, where the person is chronically predisposed to react with alarm in a range of situations (Spielberger, 1975). Females more often report performance anxiety than males in epidemiological and community studies, but the sexes are either equally represented in clinical samples or else men predominate. In the latter case, researchers suggest that men may be more inclined to seek treatment when they are unable to carry out their expected social roles (Barlow & Liebowitz, 1995). No studies have tested this assumption in the performing arts, where both men and women share a strong vocational commitment.

### Diagnosing Stage Fright

Be aware that the performer's symptoms of anxiety can be caused by the physiological effects of an illegal substance or medication or another mental disorder. Consequently, it is important to rule out organic diseases with similar symptoms, such as drug and alcohol withdrawal syndromes, hypoglycemic reactions, and major depressive episodes. In depression, anxiety symptoms and social avoidance are common but state-related, and diminish when the depression remits. Medical conditions, such as stuttering, may also cause anxiety because of their social impact; however, this problem in and of itself is not diagnosed as a social phobia. Finally, shyness is often associated with discomfort in social situations without necessarily leading to crippling symptoms. I often ask performers with stage fright to get a medical evaluation, as numerous physical conditions can affect the endocrine, metabolic, and autoimmune systems, resulting in anxiety.

In diagnosing social phobia, I look for people who exhibit a marked and persistent fear of one or more performance situation, where they anticipate acting in a way that will be humiliating or embarrassing (e.g., show symptoms of anxiety). If exposed to the feared event, this would almost invariably provoke intense anxiety, and it might even take the form of a situationally bound or predisposed panic attack. It would be reasonable to be anxious if the performer was unprepared to audition for a part, but I would diagnose social phobia if the person recognizes the fear as both excessive and unrealistic. Children are not always able to make this distinction.

Social phobia often leads to avoidance of feared events, although some performers may force themselves to perform in spite of their feelings of dread. There is also clinical impairment, due to anxious anticipation, avoidance or distress. For example, I see performers who frequently report disruptions in their normal routine, occupational functioning, or social activities, or are markedly distressed at having the phobia. Students under the age of 18 may experience problems but do not get a diagnosis unless the symptoms have persisted for at least six months, because transient social anxiety or avoidance is common in childhood and adolescence.

Finally, it helps to review a list of social and performance situations, because people rarely report the full range of their social fears without further questioning. Performers who lack social skills often show severe impairment in the work and social arenas. When they fear both public and social events, I give the specifier of generalized Social Phobia, because anxiety is attached to most social situations. Sometimes, it may be appropriate to consider an additional diagnosis of Avoidant Personality Disorder.

## Patterns of Anxiety

Like all forms of anxiety, the impact of stage fright is multi-faceted, involving cognitive, physiological, and behavioral components. These factors are partially independent with low intercorrelations, except under extreme duress; thus, it is imperative to determine if the symptoms predominate in one area, or in all of the above in order to determine the best line of treatment (Lehrer, 1987).

Interestingly, each pattern seems to represent a different kind of anxiety in performers. For example, the person most afraid of performing on stage may not be the one who refuses to go before an audience, nor show the greatest increase in heart rate or palm sweating. Of course, once it becomes a problem, stage fright can dominate the performer's life. Although amateurs and students appear to be more vulnerable than professionals (Steptoe & Fidler, 1987), the problem is obviously of concern to anyone whose job is on the line. In a survey of 2,212 members of the International Conference of Symphony and Opera Musicians, 24% of these musicians reported stage fright as a primary health complaint (Fishbein et al., 1988).

## Cognitive Factors

As already seen, certain cognitive factors can interfere with performance if left unaddressed (Burns, 1980; Lehrer, 1987; Steptoe & Fidler, 1987). These include

**TABLE 4.0  Cognitive Distortions in Performance Anxiety**

—Equating mistakes during auditions and/or performances with total failure.

—Interpreting ambiguous reactions from others as negative without sufficient evidence.

—Magnifying the importance of errors or problems should they occur (catastrophic thinking); downplaying personal assets.

—Assuming that one's adverse feelings are an accurate reflection of reality (e.g., I feel like a phony, therefore I am).

self-defeating thought patterns that distort reality, as well as negative reactions to areas where control is lacking, such as theater conditions or physical anxiety (see Table 4.0). The perception that the stakes are high and the chances for success are low can also heighten the performer's anxiety. Many of these characteristics are intrinsic to performing, which typically involves stressful work in the presence of others. However, the unpredictable nature of a live performance, coupled with the intense competition, is also a problem, because the performer must go on stage without the benefit of knowing the final outcome.

Although focusing on the self and the potential for disaster is likely to cause problems, attention can be used as a key to the solution. For example, cognitive therapy is a useful treatment modality for stage fright, because it can correct negative self-statements and target self-defeating thought patterns (Clark & Agras, 1991). This approach often involves using a diary to pinpoint irrational thoughts, while substituting constructive statements that more accurately reflect reality.

Other techniques, such as "paradoxical intention," are also useful for specific symptoms. I will ask the performer to imagine the worst case scenario in order to cope with this potential threat more effectively. Lastly, I always like to remind performers that anxiety is a normal reaction to performing and is rarely visible to others, so that they may be less frightened of their arousal and self-critical of the way they feel.

## Physiological Factors

During times of anxiety or stress, nature has designed a physiological reflex that formerly helped humans to flee or attack a hidden enemy. Unfortunately, this reaction can impair the delicate balance involved in peak performance on stage. Symptoms include perspiring (to help the person move faster); increased muscle tension (to form a body armor); greater blood flow to the large muscles, which produces cold hands and indigestion; and an increased sensitivity to small noises or movements, which leads to hypervigilance. Other reactions include heart palpitations, hyperventilation, dryness in the mouth, tremors, and nausea. I know one ballet dancer from a national company who habitually vomited before every performance until finally seeking treatment.

Fortunately, performers can learn to detect and relax low levels of muscle tension that are not needed in a particular task. For a violinist, this might mean learning to relax the tension in the forearms; dancers, on the other hand, might refrain from standing at full readiness on demi-pointe. This behavioral technique, which is known as differential relaxation, is different from progressive relaxation, which lowers arousal and may be counterproductive in a performance (Wolfe, 1989).

In contrast, debilitating physical symptoms that occur prior to a performance often respond well to psychological techniques, such as yoga, t'ai chi chuan (i.e., an ancient Chinese discipline), self-hypnosis, progressive muscle relaxation, and certain aspects of the Feldenkrais and Alexander techniques (Lehrer, 1987).

In terms of medication, researchers have found that the performer's intermittent use of beta-blockers can improve judges' ratings of a musical performance, as well as bow control, rhythm, memory, and tempo (Lehrer et al., 1987). This may not be appropriate for singers whose work calls for a certain athletic stamina because of the drug's accompanying decrease in heart rate (Gates, Saegert, Wilson, Johnson, Shepherd, & Hearne, 1985). There is also some concern that beta-blockers may reduce a performance's intensity.

## Behavioral Factors

It should not be surprising that there is a behavioral component of stage fright that must be addressed because fear can stop some performers in their tracks. Besides being unable to assert themselves or deal with emotions, such as anger, they can have problems working with teachers, stage hands, colleagues, and managers. Of course, technical problems can also cause performers to avoid practice or professional engagements, which is why I always spend time evaluating their training experiences.

Treatment for the behavioral component of stage fright may include assertiveness training and/or interventions aimed at improving technique through private study. If the level of technical mastery remains a problem, I may explore with the performer the possibility of changing to a different vocation.

Experience is also important in a performance situation. For example, music students who have studied an instrument for six or more years tend to perform better in high-anxiety situations than in those that are low in anxiety (Hamann, 1982; Hamann & Sobaje, 1983), whereas professional experience is associated with greater confidence and less nervousness and apprehension on stage (Wolfe, 1989). Typically, the anxiety of more experienced performers tends to peak right before their entrance on stage and then dissipate after several minutes.

Experience, however, can be a double-edged sword. In general, most performers spend their time practicing alone or in a classroom, with only occasional moments on stage, when they are suddenly thrown into the glare of the spotlight. Consequently, if performances are spaced too far apart, research shows that anxiety may increase; an experience known as the "incubation effect" (McAllister & McAllister, 1967). The best schedule for keeping anxiety at bay is to work at regular intervals.

If they do not have stage work, I encourage performers to arrange mini engagements in front of others according to their comfort level. This technique, known as successive approximation, begins with performing in an informal setting for a small group of friends. As the performer's confidence increases, we then discuss ways to increase both the size and the formality of the setting. If performance anxiety is a problem, then massed practice sessions scheduled two to three times a week for several months may be helpful (Lehrer, 1987).

Apart from the occasional need for vocational counseling, many technical problems can improve with guided mastery from a good teacher and repeated practice at a higher rate of difficulty (i.e., "in vivo flooding") than the task demands. Therefore, rather than focusing solely on the symptoms of performance anxiety, whether they are behavioral, cognitive, or physiological, this group also benefits from being overprepared.

## Case 4.0
## The Case of Leon

"Leon" is a 47-year-old male television actor who came to see me because of his terror of performing on stage. At our first meeting, he emanated a strong, engaging presence, which deteriorated as soon as he began speaking about his fears. As he saw it, the precipitating event for his current state of distress was landing a major role in the middle of a Broadway run. He reported that he was unable to handle the strain of being on stage six nights a week, and he was seriously thinking about leaving the play.

Each evening, besieged by terror, he was sure that he would do something to humiliate himself, which was in direct contrast to the positive feedback that he had received for his performance from the director, critics, and the audience. Even though Leon recognized that his fear did not match reality, he still was unable to cope with the situation.

Leon was also convinced that everyone knew about his stage fright, even though his physical symptoms were mild, and he had no serious behavioral problems that impaired his performance. In fact, his main area of dysfunction lay in his considerable subjective distress, which he attempted to quell by overpracticing, but it only served to heighten his self-doubts by the evening performance. Leon would then obsess about the enormity of making a mistake on a Broadway stage, and how this event would end his future prospects in the entertainment industry.

Leon held other false assumptions about his performance, which compounded his misery, most notable that it should be flawless for someone who was as experienced as himself. Consequently, he would magnify the importance of minor imperfections in his performance and analyze colleagues' casual comments for implied criticism. After the performance, he would berate himself for making mistakes.

In reviewing Leon's history, I discovered that he had always been apprehensive about performing in front of others, a fear that could be traced to the negative evaluations of his father, whom Leon described as an overbearing executive who verbally abused him as a child for even minor flaws. His mother provided no comfort during these times and was generally cold and unavailable.

Leon responded to these early family influences by becoming an overachiever in school; he would obsess for hours over his homework assignments, and rework his answers until they were "perfect." A childhood problem with stuttering increased his fear of criticism and how he would be perceived by others. Although Leon eventually overcame this condition by going to a voice therapist, he continued to fear that he might stutter on stage and sought a career in television, where retakes were possible.

In television Leon felt less vulnerable, because he knew that he would be able to correct any flaws that might lead to embarrassment or humiliation. Auditions, however, were a source of considerable stress. In the past, Leon had handled his stage fright by drinking a couple of beers and relying on a close network of friends for support when his anxiety threatened to overwhelm him. These coping mechanisms were insufficient to quell his anxiety when he was required to perform before a live audience on Broadway.

During therapy, I was not at all surprised when Leon spoke of his fears of falling short with me, worrying that he would be a less-than-perfect patient. I did my best to reassure him that there were no right or wrong behaviors and that the only goal was to give him the "tools" to cope with his situation on stage. Following mutually agreed upon goals, I divided treatment into two stages: 1) to teach Leon basic anxiety management techniques derived from cognitive-behavioral therapy, and 2) to help him reach a decision about whether he wished to remain in the play. I expected that as Leon became more able to master the performance situation, he would be in a better position to judge his role in the show.

I began by teaching Leon about the characteristics of self-assessment activities, cognitive restructuring, and anxiety management in a format that then changed to a more open forum where he could analyze his efforts at dealing with his anxiety alone. I took this approach in order to help Leon take a more active role in identifying and solving his problems in contrast to the passive approach often fostered in performing arts training programs. I also asked Leon to keep a diary of his automatic thoughts and to begin to conceptualize his problems differently. He learned how to use cognitive techniques to correct his negative self-statements and "thought-stopping" to reduce his anticipatory anxiety.

As he began to pinpoint his erroneous beliefs, such as having to be perfect, Leon was able to address the problems that could arise during a performance. For example, Leon's fear of stuttering often caused him to rush his words unnecessarily, even though this vocal problem had never happened on stage. We determined that, because his role gave him a certain amount of creative license, he could use this freedom to insert pauses as needed. This strategy allowed him to feel more in control over his performance.

We also evaluated Leon's daily schedule and his nervous habit of practicing his lines, which I saw as self-defeating because it only served to reinforce his doubts. To distract him, we scheduled other activities, such as seeing friends and engaging in sports to relieve some tension. We then arranged a quiet time one hour before the show began each evening where Leon could meditate, relax, and begin to collect his thoughts for the task at hand.

Leon responded positively to this structured approach to his performance anxiety and quickly reported a marked decrease in his subjective discomfort. After two months of psychotherapy, he was able to experience a growing sense of confidence and even to hope that the play would continue for another season. Although he still experienced moderate anxiety prior to the show, this decreased several minutes after he went on stage. He handled the minor problems that arose without resorting to catastrophic thinking. I used the final month of therapy to consolidate Leon's gains and address issues related to preventing a relapse.

## Treatment and Prevention

As we have seen, performance anxiety is a social phobia that is pathological only when it leads to marked distress and/or a disruption in functioning. It is important to know about the cognitive, physiological, and behavioral components of stage fright in order to develop the most effective treatment plan.

I believe that performing arts programs can help to prevent stage fright by taking a more realistic approach to the learning process. Students need to know that performing is difficult, and that it is normal to become anxious before an event. They also could benefit from knowledge of coping skills to reduce stress, which might be included in the standard curriculum.

If and when rejection occurs during competitions, training programs could also contribute to the student's resiliency by: a) providing constructive feedback for the refusal, and b) doing so in a private setting. Performers with technical problems could benefit from remedial training to correct bad habits.

Once performance anxiety occurs, the best approach to treating the behavioral aspect of this condition is exposure, which means encouraging the person to perform rather than to avoid the distressing situation. I often used a symptom-focused approach for cases that had the most recent occurrence, but not use it in a situation where debilitating anxiety exists prior to entering the workforce (Lowman, 1993). In the latter case, it is useful to know if the performer's anxious mood is part of a more pervasive problem, associated with a major depressive or anxiety disorder (Fava, Grandi, Canestrari, & Molnar, 1990). Traditional psychotherapy works best here, as well as in cases where the clinician suspects a strong element of secondary gain (e.g., the dysfunction protects the performer from experiencing failure or humiliation), or when dealing with the occasionally career-ending consequences of performance anxiety.

Prior attempts at self-medication must also be ferreted out because a problem with substance abuse may require an adjunctive treatment approach. If performers are using beta-blockers, they need to know the possible risks and be referred for medical supervision. As the person learns to control the various aspects of anxiety, self-defeating patterns that accompany the quest for approval and the pursuit of perfection should subside.

The following chapter reviews a subject that is often considered taboo among performers: occupational injuries and impending retirement. For most, being unable to perform is a heart-wrenching experience that strikes at the core of their identities.

# 5

# Occupational Injuries and Retirement

P erforming artists often experience a number of occupational injuries that can reduce their longevity in this career (Hamilton, 1997). Besides dealing with the hazards of special effects, the pressures of this profession may lead to burnout and repetitive stress disorders. Performers who are sidelined because of occupational problems are also emotionally vulnerable, particularly if they face the prospect of retirement. Both substance abuse and suicidal thoughts can increase markedly during this time (Hamilton & Hamilton, 1991). This chapter looks at job-related stress and the struggle that both students and professionals face when they ask the question: Is there life after performing?

## WORK HAZARDS AMONG PERFORMERS

Contrary to the public's perceptions, work conditions in a theater and film set are far from glamorous. I have already discussed the vagaries of a performing arts career, yet I wonder how many people in the audience consider that performers often experience high levels of noise, wetness, heat, light or cold? Poor ventilation and special effects, such as fog or smoke, also make for a fairly inhospitable environment when contracts do not limit the performer's exposure to such ploys.

Of course, even with a union contract, performing can be difficult. I remember swallowing gobs of paper snowflakes during the snow scene in the annual production of *The Nutcracker*, and slipping backstage because of the residue from the fog in *A Midsummer Night's Dream.* A second-degree ankle sprain and a cast kept me away from the stage for two months!

The list of problems does not stop here. Work conditions in the arts may cause a number of harmful physical reactions, although health concerns will vary according to the vocational demands within each art form.

In general, dancers are more likely to report musculoskeletal problems because of the athletic demands of their technique, whereas visual-media artists often suffer from exposure to toxic materials in their art supplies. Musicians, whether they are orchestral players or heavy-metal rockers, may have permanent hearing loss from high sound levels and may suffer physical strains if instruments do not "fit" the performers. Singers, in contrast, complain of respiratory problems and difficulties with the ear, nose and throat. Hopefully they do not have to sing with a mouthful of snowflakes.

Well-known artists in the past have suffered from work hazards as well. Some physicians suggest that Van Gogh and Goya were actually poisoned by their lead-based paints, and that even as recently as the 1960s, Eva Hess, the sculptor, may have developed fatal brain cancer from working with plastic resin. Then there is Robert Shumann, the 19th-century composer and pianist, who struggled with focal dystonia in his right hand from performing. Did this contribute to his ensuing mental problems, as some writers suggest?

The fact is that all performers are subject to a common set of hazards and anxieties at work, as well as problems related to specific occupational demands. This is why health care professionals who work with this population need to be aware of the performer's life behind the scenes.

## Occupational Demands

To get a better idea of the pressures that many professionals face today, a group of leading dancers and musicians in New York (N=48) were asked to complete a manual measuring occupational stress, strain, and coping (Hamilton et al., 1995). The measurements were looking for the type and degree of occupational stress, how performers were coping with these pressures, and whether differences existed between dancers and musicians.

First, female performers were looked at. The results showed that the women suffered from significant levels of job-related stress in dance and music due to erratic work schedules and personal isolation. However, the dancers had extra pressure in two areas: They experienced conflicting demands from their ballet masters (each of whom had their own agenda); and, they experienced confusion about the criteria used in their professional evaluations.

On the positive side, these women practiced good health habits and reported fewer mood problems than average. As leading performers, they were also less stressed due to a poor vocational attitude (i.e., they loved their work), supervisory responsibilities (i.e., they had none), and lack of success. Finally, female dancers reported fewer physical illnesses than the norm.

The men's results portrayed a much bleaker picture in the performing arts. Whereas all the men suffered from erratic work schedules, this problem was most severe for male dancers, who are less utilized in a ballet company than ballerinas. Still, similarities between the sexes in dance existed in the areas of ambiguous professional evaluations and mixed messages from their ballet masters—both of which added to the level of occupational stress.

Coping strategies were less than adequate when they were compared to the general population. The men in both art forms were depressed, anxious, and irritable; their personal relationships were highly conflicted; and they reported a number of health concerns, including weight fluctuations, sleep problems, and overuse of alcohol. In addition, only male musicians practiced good health habits. And both the dancers and musicians lacked social support and did not rely on cognitive coping skills as frequently as the average man. The only good news for male performers was their positive attitude toward their vocation, and a lack of supervisory responsibilities.

What do these results mean? Obviously, performing is not a "9-to-5" job; musicians can freelance in the Bronx one day and Long Island the next to try to make a living. But dancers often learn their daily schedule the night before when the rehearsals are posted for the following day. As we have seen, additional sources of occupational stress also occur in dance, which exerts its own unique constraints.

In general, the artistic personnel in dance companies are notorious for making inexplicable casting changes, leaving many dancers bewildered about their value as performers and prospects for promotion. Adding to the confusion are well-meaning ballet masters, who often compensate for their subordinate position within the company hierarchy by teaching the performer to do a part (which they may have danced) "their way." Juggling these conflicting demands is stressful, because of the consequences—if you fail to please those in authority, you may not get cast, or worse. Remember, dancers are not entitled to tenure, and union contracts are renewed annually.

A final issue raised by this study is men's health concerns and men's limited ability to cope with stress, which was significant. Although the focus was not specifically on illness, it is possible that these problems are linked, at least in part, to the AIDS epidemic. In a recent survey of a small group of male dancers (N=18), 48% stated they were homosexual, 56% had been tested for the HIV virus and, of this group, 10% tested positive (Hamilton, 1996). Clearly, we need to do further research on AIDS if we are to meet the psychological needs of performers.

## Coping with Burnout

Over time, performers may also suffer burnout, which usually happens when they have to comply with extremely high standards at work (Burke & Kirchmeyer, 1990). The most obvious signs of burnout in overworked performers are feeling emotionally exhausted, depersonalized, and unsuccessful. Burnout can also lower self-esteem, making it more difficult to be objective about one's work and be realistic about what can be accomplished (Golembiewski & Kim, 1989).

A major cause for burnout is occupational stress, resulting from unclear role demands, too many demands, and conflicts with others. This is especially true when it is coupled with real or perceived lack of control over work and limited social support from one's supervisors.

Interestingly, too many and too few demands on the job can lead to physical symptoms and psychological strain (Osipow & Spokane, 1983). In the entertainment industry, this can happen when the "big break" comes a little too fast, or the performer is unclear as to what the next move should be. The following cases, although very different, highlight the problems that arise from burnout.

## Case 5.0
## The Overnight Success

A 22-year-old actor suffered from role overload after a catastrophic experience on a national tour. By all accounts, it should have been a happy story, as this actor had walked into a leading role right after graduating from college. His talent landed him the part even though his predecessor was a well-known star. The problem was that the demands of the job soon exceeded his personal resources. In each city of their tour, the critics compared his performance to the former lead, while the show's manager stressed that the success of the entire production lay on his shoulders. Alcohol, drugs, and a premature retirement followed, even though roles continued to be offered to him in television and on the stage. Success was the source of his distress rather than the answer to his problems.

The opposite scenario occurs when a job is not clearly defined like when the performer has no clear sense of what to do to "get ahead." Time after time, whether it is an audition or a change in casting, I find professionals grappling with the $64,000 dollar question, WHY? Without an answer—and harboring concerns about being ignored—performers often become riddled with doubt about their ability to have an impact on or to evoke a response from others. The longer that their needs for recognition and success go unmet, the more likely they are to experience significant narcissistic vulnerability. This is marked by experiences of acute self-consciousness, a tendency toward shame, and painful questions about self-worth.

This was the case for a dancer who came to see me after suffering serious damage to her self-esteem.

## Case 5.1
## Left in the Wings

This 37-year-old modern dancer had performed in an internationally known company for a decade, dancing choice roles and choreographing on her own. While most ballet careers are winding down at this stage, modern dancers often perform well into their 30s and early 40s because of a less taxing technique. Consequently, the setting had seemed ideal; this dancer could perform, while slowly gaining experience as a choreographer that would help her in a career transition. The shock came when the artistic director's health began to fail and she fell out of favor with her assistant who took over most of the day-to-day activities. Slowly but surely, he took away her special roles, humiliated her in rehearsals, and refused to give her opportunities to choreograph. As this professional's despondency grew, she began to think about retiring from dance. Injuries and a clinical depression eventually led her to seek psychotherapy. The result was that she began to choreograph outside of the company, while utilizing the name recognition of the company to get sponsorship.

As we see, the overcommitment pattern manifested in many performers, as well as too many and too few demands, can lead to burnout, injuries, and substance abuse. I help these individuals achieve more of a balance between work and leisure activities, while attending to their physical and emotional needs. Helping them think differently about their problems is particularly useful when their self-worth is tied solely to achievement. Lastly, performers often benefit from stress-management techniques and relaxation exercises to reduce anxiety.

## REACTIONS TO INJURIES

Part of the problem for professionals who face unsympathetic management is the fact that the supply of talent in the performing arts greatly exceeds the demand. No one feels comfortable being "out," because there is always an understudy waiting in the wings, ready and eager to take your place. By demanding perfection and increasingly high standards of athleticism, the performing arts creates physical stress that can lead to overuse syndromes and disability.

The classic performer's leit motiv of "no pain no gain" causes many insecure professionals to practice passages over and over until they bleed. Injuries are also on the rise, as professionals follow more demanding schedules and perform more difficult repertory.

Overuse syndromes—the bugaboo of many talented artists—can result from practicing a piece incessantly for a show or attempting to go beyond the performer's level of expertise without sufficient technical preparation. Among the different art forms, the most athletic is obviously dance. Let us see how these performers fair over time.

### Physical Stress

A survey of a large group of dancers (N=960) found that overuse problems, such as tendonitis (39%), chronic injuries (52%), and arthritis (15%), are fairly common (Hamilton, 1997). Lack of strength also appears to be a factor during training;

female dancers with hip problems and tendonitis are more likely to begin pointe work before the age of 12 rather than after this age. Men, in turn, have significantly more shoulder problems than women (28% vs 7%), probably from partnering and lifts.

The dilemma for dancers, as well as other types of performers, is that the more years they practice, the greater their chance of developing injuries. In the present study, chronic injuries are significantly higher in professionals (61%) and ex-dancers (66%) compared to older (46%) or younger (47%) dance students. Arthritis, a crippling disease, is common among ballet and modern dancers. Finally, dancers who work for 18 years or longer report more injuries in every category versus those who dance for less than a decade.

What do dancers do when they get injured? Remember, pain is often associated with progress in the performing arts, especially in overachievers. The results show that 9 out of 10 dancers (89%) handle their injuries alone; 60% seek medical help only when they can no longer dance full-out; and almost half (49%) continue to work in spite of being injured. Dancers whose injuries keep them from reaching their goals experience significantly more symptoms of performance anxiety than those without this problem. These symptoms include constant fear when dancing in front of others (19% vs 11%) and bodily sensations of anxiety (22% vs 10%).

## Less is Sometimes More

To find out what is wrong with this picture, ask any reputable orthopedist in performing arts medicine. You will learn, as I did, that overuse injuries respond best to modified activities that favor the disability and to rest. Injured performers also benefit from medical services, such as supervised physical therapy and other treatment modalities, as well as the use of medications when appropriate. Injuries are not a time to tough it out on your own!

Unfortunately, the psychological drive to be perfect often underlies performers' destructive work habits, especially in those who perceive a mismatch between their real and ideal self. If you recall, personal adjustment increases as we come closer to our ideal self, whereas shame reflects the sense of deflation that follows our inability to measure up. Under these circumstances, the remedy is often to work harder, with unfavorable results if this occurs regardless of injuries.

Rather than focusing on perfection, performers do best when they validate their efforts to improve by working with—not against—their bodies. Many also need to put their work role in a broader context, while moving away from overly ambitious strivings that are a dead end. In my monthly advice column in *Dance Magazine*, I have the difficult task of advising dancers without the right bodies or technique to consider other vocations that might be more fruitful, saving dance class as a special treat.

With dance professionals, the pressure to perform before injuries have healed can lead to a history of chronic pain affecting an entire arm or leg. Beyond the actual physical trauma, there may be a host of social and psychological problems

TABLE 5.0   Dancers Unjustly Criticized by their Teachers in Class

|  | Dancers | |
| --- | --- | --- |
|  | Yes | No |
| *Injury History* | | |
| Arthritis | 19% | 11%** |
| Stress fx | 21% | 11%** |
| Chronic injs. | 59% | 45%** |
| Tendonitis | 47% | 31%** |
| *Site of Injury* | | |
| Foot | 30% | 23%* |
| Knee | 38% | 29%** |
| Back | 28% | 17%*** |
| Hip | 26% | 14%*** |
| Ankle | 45% | 28%*** |

Note:   *p<.05 **p<.01 ***p<.001

originating from teachers, whose power continues to influence performers long after they have moved on to other mentors in this single-minded and often isolating profession.

## Teaching Practices

To a great extent, training in the performing arts is much like training in the military; teachers point out mistakes and encourage their students to keep working in the face of discomfort and pain. Although these teaching practices can be useful at times, they are also subject to abuse if taken to an extreme. Our results show that one out of four dancers (24%) report that they have been expected to keep working even with a serious injury (Hamilton, 1997). Forty-eight percent have also felt unjustly criticized by their teachers in dance class. These teaching practices have a serious effect on dancers' injury patterns and work habits.

### Unjustly Criticized

Dancers with critical teachers too often continue to work while injured significantly more than those without this type of influence (61% vs 39%). These dancers also report a higher incidence of arthritis, stress fractures, chronic injuries and tendonitis, and more foot, knee, back, hip, and ankle problems (see Table 5.0).

Later on, dancers with critical teachers were unable to achieve their goals as professionals because of problems with self-sabotage in their careers (20% vs 9%).

Not surprisingly, these dancers also sought out a number of health care providers over the years, ranging from orthopedists to psychotherapists for emotional stress.

TABLE 5.1   Dancers Expected to Work Injured by their Teachers

| | Dancers | |
|---|---|---|
| | Yes | No |
| *Injury History* | | |
| Arthritis | 21% | 13%** |
| Stress fx | 27% | 13%*** |
| Chronic injs. | 66% | 48%*** |
| Tendonitis | 52% | 34%*** |
| | | |
| *Site of Injury* | | |
| Shoulder | 12% | 7%** |
| Knee | 40% | 31%* |
| Foot | 35% | 24%** |
| Back | 36% | 19%*** |
| Hip | 33% | 16%*** |
| Ankle | 52% | 31%*** |

Note:   $*p<.05$  $**p<.01$  $***p<.001$

### Expected to Work Injured

Similar problems occur when teachers expect dancers to work with a serious injury. The results found that these dancers continue to work with physical problems (75% vs 41%), and use more support services, including psychotherapy. They also have significantly more arthritis, stress fractures, chronic problems, tendonitis, and injuries to the shoulder, knee, foot, back, hip, and ankle (see Table 5.1).

Dancers whose teachers expect them to work with a serious injury do not achieve their goals as performers. Their reasons include injuries (24% vs 14%), self-sabotage (21% vs 13%), and poor health (9% vs 2%).

## Teaching Standards

Destructive teaching practices put all performers at significant risk for injuries, particularly if these practices occur under the guise of training them to be stoic and self-critical. There is a need for change, beginning with the establishment of national teaching standards. Teachers could also benefit from required courses on kinesiology and child psychology so they can help students learn healthy work habits that contribute to their physical and mental well-being.

## THE EMOTIONAL COSTS OF INJURIES

Although the consequences of a serious injury can be profound for all patients, the stakes are detrimental for the violinist with carpal tunnel syndrome or the dancer with a torn ACL whose livelihood, not to mention self-esteem, is on the line. Remember, this is a profession where 62% of performers do not have full-time jobs (U.S. Census, 1990), and even professionals with steady work, such as orchestral musicians, must reaudition at intervals to keep their union contract. Considering these harsh realities, a debilitating injury represents a dilemma of major proportions.

## The Injured Psyche

Beyond the pain to the performer's body and the loss of income, the most disturbing element of an injury is being unable to practice one's art form. As with other dedicated professionals, it is the process of regularly engaging in meaningful activity (practice) that is truly rewarding to the performer, not just the annual recital or getting a glowing review in *The New York Times.*

This intrinsic enjoyment in the performing arts is based on physical mastery of one's "instrument," with little or no separation between who one is as a person and the ability to perform. The result is that, rather than just losing their health when they are injured, they may also feel that they have lost their identities.

Performers suffer an added blow if their injury separates them from colleagues in the community. Even the unemployed spend time primarily in the company of other performers, making the rounds of auditions and taking classes to stay in shape. This is especially true for members of a repertoire company, as well as advanced students who may work as much as 10 hours a day in class and rehearsals for an annual workshop performance.

Performers who share their experiences on a daily basis often develop significant camaraderie with their colleagues. With few resources to fall back on outside of their profession, those who become injured are at a distinct disadvantage. They will be isolated from their peers and have to confront the process of recovery alone.

Considering these factors, performers who experience work dysfunctions because of age, illness, or injury are particularly vulnerable to psychological distress. Still, a serious setback means different things to different people. Besides individual variations in personality dynamics, job-related problems can remove the performer from failures and defeats, as well as the rewards derived from this work. These differences make it difficult to predict how each person will respond during recovery—even with the same injury!

More complex reactions to being injured may also interfere with the process of recovery (Krueger, 1981). For example, it is typical for Equity performers who injure themselves in a musical to receive disability payments after they lose their jobs. Because the chances of getting another position in a show are slim, health care professionals often find that this group takes longer to heal, basically prolonging their recovery for financial reasons.

Performers who use a disability to excuse failure or the inability to thrive in this career can make recovery from the injury worse. It is noteworthy that a follow-up study (mean = 7.5 years) of dancers who had undergone surgery for posterior ankle pain showed a disproportionate number of the "fair" and "poor" results in the amateur dancers rather than the professional dancers (Hamilton, Geppert, & Thompson, 1996). The authors speculated that the amateurs' need to "explain" their lack of status in the profession contributed to their unsatisfactory outcome.

It is difficult to get a handle on the emotional responses to trauma, particularly because each case is different. A new trend among rehabilitation teams is to rely increasingly on clinical psychologists for testing, consultation, clinical work, program planning, research, and training along with other health care workers (Fordyce, 1981; Lechner, 1994).

## Stages of Rehabilitation

Once musculoskeletal injuries occur, the performer must pass through several consecutive stages during the healing process in order to regain motion, strength, endurance, and timing. Depending on where the performer is in the healing process will affect the performer's emotional adjustment to the injury and determine the rate of recovery (Krueger, 1981).

Psychological factors that can impede recovery generally fall into two categories: 1) prior emotional problems that interfere with physical rehabilitation, and 2) current adjustment problems to the injury, leading to depression, hostility, or basic noncompliance.

### The Initial Stage of Recovery

As with any traumatic event, the immediate reaction to an acute injury is often shock. The injured performer is caught completely off guard and usually cannot yet comprehend the scope or severity of the disability on his or her life. Although this reaction rarely lasts more than a few hours, denial—which is one component of shock—often continues (Krueger, 1981).

Denial is adaptive at this stage because, besides preserving the performer's self-concept, it promotes the hope that recovery will be swift and smooth. Thus, the person does not reject the reality of the injury so much as its importance and possible long-term limitations. But this defense can become maladaptive over time if it fails to diminish and interferes with recovery (i.e., the person refuses appropriate treatment).

In most cases, injured performers begin to confront the meaning of the injury on their lives as medical care commences, a situation that can initiate a painful period of mourning (Krueger, 1981; Lerman, 1979). Although it is natural to grieve following a loss in functioning, this response can be frustrating for the rehabilitation team. Even injured performers with no preexisting psychopathology may become unmotivated, hostile, or withdrawn after denial abates.

The most important task at this stage is to help the performer think in concrete terms and discover the actual—although limited—choices that exist. Personal attention from significant others is also crucial. In sports, social support has been found to be the most important aspect in keeping injured athletes in a minimum six-week rehab program (Fisher, Domm, & Wuest, 1988). The injured performer will also profit from a reassuring routine in physical therapy, as well as a new peer group made up of other injured performers.

### The Intermediate Stage of Recovery

I usually see the performer's frame of mind improve by the middle stage of recovery, which is associated with the first tangible signs of progress. Still, a sense of personal accomplishment is only available to those who learn to enjoy the small victories connected with healing, because there are still obvious physical limitations. Psychological problems that require further assessment at this point may be overt (e.g., substance abuse and clinical depression) or represent more complex reactions that interfere with rehabilitation (e.g., procrastination during rehab).

It helps to remind injured performers that it is normal to experience a certain amount of pain and stiffness during recovery, as well as minor setbacks along the way. I also employ cognitive strategies if they are predisposed to think the worst (e.g., "I'm sure to reinjure myself") in order to help them cope more effectively with their fears. This is a time when performers can also lift their spirits by focusing on body conditioning to avoid getting out of shape. Various possibilities include Pilates, Feldenkrais, and Alexander techniques; non-impact aerobics (e.g., swimming) that restore stamina and maintain weight; and remedial classes that evaluate faulty work habits.

My goal in directing performers' attention to healthy avenues of pursuit is to help them to feel more secure, making them less likely to focus on the possible negative consequences of the injury to their career. When all is said and done, performers who adapt during recovery are more likely to set up conditions in which the injury becomes a catalyst for personal renewal.

### The Advanced Stage of Recovery

The last phase of injury rehabilitation is self-sustaining; performers have resumed practice and class, and it is clear that they will be able to work once again. The injury, however, is still in recovery as they slowly regain full stamina and coordination, which is why they must guard against prematurely throwing themselves back into a full schedule. Many performers reinjure themselves, even if they are fully reconditioned and ready to discard old habits, if they play catch up.

Performers can also get into trouble in this final phase by cutting back on their physical therapy, which could sabotage all their efforts. At this point, it helps to remind them to focus on realistic goals, based on their physician's advice, in order to avoid setting themselves up for reinjury. To curb their frustrations, they also need to remain close to prior systems of support, such as physical therapy or Pilates, where there is minimal stress of competition.

Another potential problem for injured professionals during recovery is losing valued roles to others. Time most likely will rectify this loss, too, as long as they are patient and remain injury-free. Meanwhile, they can enjoy being back with their peers and reentering the rewarding routine of their art form.

## Conclusion

Injured performers are particularly vulnerable to psychological stress because of the many profound changes that a disability wreaks on their body-image, lifestyle and abilities. Consequently, I often encourage injured performers to find substitutes for productive activity and sources of self-esteem. For example, it is possible for performers to use this respite from their work to explore other interests or even to resume an aborted education. Besides giving them an advantage in the event of a career transition, these activities reinforce other aspects of their evolving identities. Performers who are concerned about weight gain following an injury can also meet regularly with a registered dietician.

Recovering from an injury can be a constructive experience for those who adapt to the various stages of physical rehabilitation. Performers who find themselves unable to cope with anxiety or depression should receive outside counseling as an adjunct to the rehabilitative process.


## RELINQUISHING THE DREAM: MOURNING AND RELEASE

Sooner or later, all performers face the dreaded day when it is finally time to give up the dream. Elisabeth Kubler-Ross, a noted expert on dying, has referred to this moment of retirement as one of the little deaths of life (Kubler-Ross, 1975). This is especially true for performers, who may have spent three-quarters of their lives working in this profession.

In my own career, the reality of retiring hit me at the age of 26 (I had started dance at 8 years old), after a serious injury and a messy divorce. Suddenly, there was no Prince Charming to take me away on his horse, and my days of performing were numbered—most dancers are retired from a company in their early 30s. Thankfully, Peter Martins, the new director of the New York City Ballet, let me leave gradually. It took 10 years of full-time study to become a licensed clinical psychologist, eight of which occurred in school while I was still performing with the company. To get the ball rolling, I took my high school equivalency exam. When I passed that with flying colors, I figured anything was possible.

Without my education, I would have been in the same boat as many performers—lost and lacking a job. For the most part, traditional training programs in the performing arts promote a narrow vocationalism, leaving many performers with few resources outside of this profession. Making a career change could then be emotionally devastating, even for the very young. Retiring performers come to a crossroad. To proceed they must achieve a new definition of self.

What should performers expect during a career transition? In Tatelbaum's book, *The Courage to Grieve* (1980), we learn that it is common for people to experience a mixture of raw and often contradictory feelings following a profound personal loss. In fact, professionals often report anger, relief, regret, sorrow, euphoria, and fear during various stages of retirement (Lindner, 1990). Performers may also feel that they are losing their identity, making the transition process especially difficult to manage.

Another factor to consider in retirees is their motivation for leaving this career. Are they reaching out for a more attractive alternative, or are they being forced out by default, because they are unemployed, burned out, tired of touring, or need to be practical about their future? By the time I left dancing, I loved my new profession in psychology and was ready to take the plunge. However, performers who wait until their 40s to reassess where they are going are often paralyzed by fear. Remember, this is a profession without rules; Tony award winners still have to audition for work, and job opportunities are scarce.

Many performers who retire from this profession lose their primary, if not only, source of self-esteem. Those who are unable to cope with the stress of this event and restore narcissistic equilibrium will experience strain manifested in psychological problems, such as mood changes, or physical illness (Lowman, 1993).

The results from a survey of performers highlight some of the emotional difficulties that surround the prospect of retirement (Hamilton & Hamilton, 1991). Questionnaires were distributed to 35 women, requesting detailed information on their personal habits, injury history, retirement plans, and mental status. These performers had embarked on a professional career before the age of 20 after training for a minimum of seven years, a fact that reflects their deep emotional investment in performing.

The results showed significant differences for those performers who had been forced to stop working over the past year because of a serious orthopedic problem. First, injured performers used more illicit and prescribed drugs, as well as more alcohol, than performers without a physical disability. Surprisingly, 38% also reported that they had actually considered suicide as their self-worth deteriorated. No incidence of suicidal thoughts was reported in the healthy performers. The prospect of retirement was also significantly related to impaired psychological functioning. Performers who were contemplating retirement used a higher proportion of drugs, which included marijuana, tranquilizers, and sleeping pills. They also reported thinking more about suicide.

Again, it is important to remember that everyone's response to stress will differ; personal variables, such as self-esteem and locus of control (whether a person thinks his or her actions are determined by external or internal events) will affect how one copes (Lowman, 1993). In addition, performers who feel optimistic and in charge of their lives do better after an injury occurs than those who perceive few options (Hamilton, 1997).

## The Process of Mourning

Retiring from performing brings on a painful period of mourning, as the performer comes to grips with a whole series of losses in the workplace, in the community and, most of all, in his or her identity. Before the person can move forward into the next phase of life, the grieving performer must: 1) come to terms with his/her past; 2) "let go" of the lost attachment to his/her art form; and 3) reinvest in life after performing.

Bypassing any of these steps during the mourning process may result in a wide range of psychological and physical problems due to unresolved grief (Tatelbaum, 1980). Fortunately, this state is usually reversible, even years later, if the performer is able to complete the stages of mourning.

## Reappraising the Past

The initial focus of a transition is on the past, as performers begin to confront what has happened to their aspirations and careers. If an acute injury forces the performer into retirement, he or she will immediately experience a period of shock and denial. Performers tell me that they often feel suspended in a state of unreality during this time, only vaguely aware of what is going on around them. Sorrow and pain are masked; however, they may lash out angrily at a variety of targets.

As denial abates, performers often find that it is easier to fully experience and express reactions to their loss. Still, conflicting feelings can arise for a variety of reasons. Successful performers may look back at their careers and feel that the best part of their lives are over, whereas disillusioned performers may be devastated by their lack of success and find it difficult to relinquish hope of ever achieving this goal. Both types of performers will experience pain and discomfort. However, their ingrained beliefs about themselves, the world, and the future will ultimately play a role in how they respond to a career transition.

Several examples may help to illustrate this point. For instance, students or professionals who believe that they are *only* performers are unlikely to explore alternate career paths as easily as "people" who love to perform. This problem is compounded by a world view that rests on the belief that power lies in the hands of others (e.g., the artistic director), because it fosters a passive approach to life. Finally, pessimists who accept the idea that a future without performing is worthless may give up hope and become depressed. These beliefs can be modified with professional help, according to the objective light of reality.

## Letting Go of Performing

As performers begin to change their beliefs and let go of their intense attachment to this career, the emphasis shifts from the past to the future. For the first time, they may feel ready to mobilize their resources apart from this vocation. Performers need to protect themselves from disappointment at this stage by having realistic expectations. After decades of pursuing one goal, they cannot find a new path immediately. In fact, real change will require a period of ambiguity, as the performer explores different interests and tries out different behaviors. This is a period of relative disorganization, in which it is normal for performers to experience conflicting feelings about the past even as they begin to face the future.

While understanding that ruminating about performing is part of the healing process, performers often require help to address unresolved guilt over lost career opportunities or residual anger at others who are not facing such a serious loss. Those who are anxious and depressed, have low self-esteem, or fear failure may procrastinate at this time (Lowman, 1993). Indications in therapy that I need to look more closely at some performers' reactions include appearing wooden or unemotional, reporting a sense of paralysis regarding a career transition, or withdrawing from others. Emotional support continues to be important, as performers struggle to initiate change without direction or authority.

A final aspect of "letting go" involves relinquishing symbols from the past, whether it is wearing one's hair in a bun or taking a vacation and leaving an instrument behind. This is a time to appreciate the skills that will be an asset outside of the performing arts, as well as to discover untapped strengths that were previously overlooked because of a busy schedule.

Typically, performers have many traits that transfer readily to another vocation. Actors tend to be great communicators; dancers are unusually goal-directed; and all performers are known for their discipline and work ethic, even if they lack a higher education. Thus, they have much to offer a new career; it is only when they get caught up in a cage of self-doubt and negative beliefs that they may ignore their full potential.

## Reinvesting in Life

The final phase of a career transition is one of recovery; the performer has met the most challenging aspects of mourning this career and survived. This is now the time to choose wisely, as well as to reconsider past decisions. For instance, the performer's first job may not be the best fit, particularly if this came about out of desperation after suffering a serious injury.

A useful technique to help performers reinvest in life at this stage is visualization, where they vividly picture themselves after this career with a family, a job, another career, or all of the above. This technique can also complement vocational counseling, which often seems initially threatening. As performers imagine themselves in the future, they are more likely to adopt a strategy to handle the concrete aspects of a career transition, such as financial planning, time-management, and a realistic appraisal of the job market.

The last point to consider during recovery is that a career transition is always an ongoing process. Performers who adapt to life after this vocation will perceive themselves in a different way, as will other people in their community. This, in turn, will require additional adjustments and change. Throughout these developments, it is important for performers to remain true to their own aspirations—the standards, ideals, and values that they have cherished in the past—because it will give them the sustenance to change and look forward to the future.

## Summary

Successful grieving requires that performers address the extensive role that this career has played in their lifestyles and identities if they are to move on. And this is painful. This aspect of the transition often unleashes a mixture of contradictory and painful feelings, which become resolved only after performers have moved through the various stages of mourning. Because everyone copes differently in the face of a profound loss, psychotherapy may be necessary for those whose sense of self remains fragile.

To accomplish a successful career transition, it is important for students and professionals to be aware of the emotional pitfalls that accompany retirement. Performers may require assistance to:

- Recognize and address underlying issues of loss;
- Modify dysfunctional and/or high risk behaviors;
- Incorporate support systems to facilitate change; and
- Adopt a proactive approach to career planning.

With the help of outside counseling and support, performers can learn to use the grieving process as a stepping stone to personal renewal. In this way, they can turn adversity into triumph and reclaim other aspects of their evolving identities.

Now that we have examined the pitfalls of performing, it is time for some solutions. In the final chapter, I will discuss the exciting new field of performing arts psychology, where the goal is to combat the pressures of this wonderful but demanding profession.

# 6

# Performing Arts Psychology

J ust like sports psychology arose to serve elite and recreational athletes (Hays & Smith, 1996), I have seen a similar birth in terms of the needs of performers, with a new focus on psychological issues in the arts. Research in this area has led to a distinct body of knowledge, in addition to a variety of clinical applications, ranging from school settings to specialty clinics (Hamilton, 1997; Harman, 1991; Kanefield, 1990). This chapter explores current concepts in the field and psychology's emerging role in the treatment of performing artists.

## DEVELOPING A PROFICIENCY

A decade ago the stresses and strains involved in the arts remained, for the most part, hidden from view. Yet times are beginning to change (Harman, 1991). Since 1985, more than 20 performing-arts medicine centers have opened their doors in such major cities as New York, Toronto, Boston, Victoria (Australia), Chicago, London, Philadelphia, and San Francisco. The goal is two-fold: first, to address the primary health needs of performers, which are similar to the general population; and next, to treat the specific problems endemic to each art form.

Catering to the special needs of performers is important, because of the unique psychological, biological, and social stresses related to this vocation. For this reason, many health care institutes have clinics for the treatment of dance injuries, specially designed examination rooms for instrumentalists and vocalists, and physical and occupational therapy geared to different groups of performers.

The advent of performing arts medicine has also led to the establishment of psychological services in health care clinics, as well as in a number of arts academies, because it is difficult to address the physical aspects of performing without taking into account the huge impact that mental processes can have on individual functioning. These services are often available on a sliding scale, which is a big step forward because many performers lack the necessary funds or health insurance to cover the costs of psychotherapy. Performers with worker's compensation are covered for job-related injuries.

The emotional toll that this career wreaks is evident to me every day in my clinical practice, as well as in the documented use of psychological services for performers. In one study conducted over a 12-month period in San Francisco, the University of California's Health Program for Performing Artists admitted 25% of its patients primarily for psychological problems, which included severe anxiety and/or depression, personality disorders, somatoform disorders, psychoses, and suicidal behavior (Ostwald & Avery, 1991).

In Canada, a longitudinal study showed that arts students are likewise susceptible to emotional stress; this group sought psychological counseling significantly more than either academically gifted or regular academic students (Robson & Gitev, 1991b). Again, sources of distress included anxiety, as well as perfectionism, performance anxiety, and feelings of inadequacy.

At the Julliard School, considered to be one of the top performing arts academies in the country, 17.5% of the undergraduates and 8.5% of the graduate students requested psychological services during the 1988-1989 academic year—a rate that may reflect a minimum estimate if students sought help outside of the premises (Kanefield, 1990). In fact, these elite students' usage of psychotherapy did increase with the establishment of the residence hall in 1991, according to the former director, because this allowed for better documentation of the need for psychotherapy (E. Kanefield, personal communication, July 1991).

An increasing number of psychotherapists with experience in the performing arts are now available to care for this population; however, there is still a long way to go in meeting the needs of the more than 350,000 professionals in this country (U.S. Census, 1990), and countless students engaged in professional training. So, where do you get training in performing arts psychology?

## Training in Psychology

Many graduate students want to know if there are doctoral programs that specialize in psychology and the arts. The answer is "no," although it is possible to acquire competence in the area by conducting research, beginning with your doctoral dissertation, and attending workshops and conferences. A formalized proficiency in performance psychology may also lie in the future. The American Psychological Association (APA)—the largest national association of psychologists in the United

States—has recently established the Committee for the Recognition of Specialties and Proficiencies in Professional Psychology.

As with all practitioners, training in the field begins with a doctoral degree in an APA-approved program. Even though none of these graduate programs specialize in the arts, completion of the degree will establish the proper foundation by focusing on the diagnosis and treatment of emotional and behavioral problems. Although training may be based on one perspective (e.g., psychodynamic) or several modalities (e.g., dynamic, cognitive, and behavioral), it should be known that treatment programs for performers often rely on a number of techniques. This diverse approach may reflect the growing trend toward psychotherapy integration in the field (Stricker & Gold, 1993).

Specific experience with performers usually occurs after psychology students complete their training and internship. The best place to gain this experience is at a performing-arts medicine clinic. Although this is rarely lucrative (i.e., fee for service), it provides invaluable experience with a wide variety of performers and job-related problems. The job titles in these facilities include assistant psychologist, or clinical psychologist after licensure has occurred.

Practitioners may also want to gain expertise in a specific area, such as eating disorders. This was my interest because I wanted to help dancers and training academies with weight issues. So, in addition to working at the Miller Institute for Performing Artists, I spent many years doing research and clinical work on eating disorders on both inpatient and outpatient units. I have also been able to use my training and background to educate the 235,000 readers of *Dance Magazine* who read my advice column each month.

As in my case, private practice is a natural career move after one has gained sufficient experience with this population. Referrals may come through word of mouth; contacting unions, such as EQUITY or SAG; or networking with physicians who treat performers. Presenting timely topics at local schools and companies is also an option (e.g., how to combat performance anxiety). Income will vary, depending on the mix of students, performers—with and without health insurance—and celebrities.

## Psychology and the Arts

Networking with colleagues provides further opportunities to continue your education. "Psychology & the Arts," which is Division 10 of the American Psychological Association, focuses exclusively on the psychological processes involved in the arts—a domain broadly construed to include the visual arts, literature, music, dance and theater, in addition to the study of creativity and eminence. Members receive discounts to specialty journals, as well as a biannual newsletter which reviews new research, books, and upcoming conferences.

Psychology and the Arts also sponsors invited addresses, symposia, papers, poster sessions, career seminars, and workshops at the annual American Psychological Association convention. Other organizations, such as the Performing Arts Medicine Association and the International Association for Dance Medicine and Science, hold annual conferences and publish professional journals devoted to the occupational problems in the performing arts. The American Association for Psychology and the Performing Arts—a new organization with roots in Europe—held its first conference in 1997.

With enough experience, the graduate student will discover that each art form selects certain areas of concentration, leading to a high degree of consistency among members, similar to other groups who undergo a long educational or apprenticeship program (Lowman, 1993). Performers also choose a particular art form and then adapt to the culture's requirements for over a decade.

It is important to know that being a dancer is not the same as being an opera singer; the criteria for selection, training, success, and longevity differ. A dancer's career is typically over by the mid 30s, whereas an opera singer may be just hitting her prime. In the first case, you are dealing with a relatively young, uneducated person who often has limited experience on which to fall back. Opera singers have greater longevity but often live with the constant fear of losing their voice—it may last into their early 60s or disappear practically overnight, depending on hormones, fatigue, or technique. Both performers experience stress, and transition to another career can be difficult; however, their backgrounds, life stages, and concerns are markedly different.

Mastery in the performing arts also differs at many levels, often leading to problems when deficits occur. For example, someone who wants to become a comedian must have timing, originality, and the ability to "work a crowd," besides being humorous. Consequently, clinicians need to differentiate between performers in dance, music, voice, drama and comedy, and between classical and popular forms.

## TREATMENT PROTOCOLS

Although knowledge of each art form's requirements can serve as a guide during treatment with this population, I try never to begin a consultation with a preconceived notion of what a performer might want or need. The reality is that therapy may be focused and relatively short-term. Or it could be open-ended and of longer duration, depending on the performer's coping skills, which are a reflection of the self.

The ability to cope has a developmental dimension, as challenges and opportunities replace previous ones throughout the lifespan. For this reason, it is impossible to evaluate the performer's coping skills apart from his or her life experiences. What may be adequate for one set of circumstances may prove to be inadequate for another set of situations.

One common problem in performers is low self-esteem, which may range from mild feelings of inferiority to self-hatred and a sense of being defective, although the grandiose performer who feels capable of doing anything can also have a coping skills deficiency. I often see this problem in successful performers who expect to generalize their accomplishments to other areas in which their talent is more modest.

Excessively high expectations for achievement, typical of many people in the performing arts, is another coping skills deficiency. The performers' expectations must take into account the fact that a career often involves disappointments, problems, loss, unfairness, and suffering—as well as access to possible joys, rewards, satisfactions, and pleasure. Individuals who do not accommodate the inevitable changes during a career-span are especially vulnerable to psychological distress.

In contrast, performers who resist the deleterious effects of stress are those who take some form of action. Examples of coping include good health habits, leisure activities, social support, and problem-solving skills, which create a balance between professional and personal priorities. If this balance does not occur, strain can arise, leading to anxiety, depression, lethargy, cardiovascular problems, disturbed sleep, over or under eating, and substance abuse. Psychological stress can also impair work and personal relationships.

### The Initial Consultation

Typically, performers who see me for psychotherapy because of work-related problems are experiencing varying degrees of psychological dysfunction. My task during the initial consultation is to determine if their symptoms preceded or followed problems at work by taking a personal history, evaluating their training and stage experiences, and judging their current level of mastery as performers. This information is necessary in deciding how to tailor treatment: Is it appropriate to focus exclusively on work, treat the psychological problems as separate or combine personal and work issues? In most cases, work and psychological problems are intertwined.

Working with performers accustomed to being watched, the therapist is often perceived as critic or admirer, depending on the individual's background. Consequently, many performers expend considerable energy trying to elicit a smile or reassuring comment, as they do in the rest of their lives. In the entertainment world, individuals often feel like failures if they do not get approval. Often, it is helpful to use this experience to tap into other areas where approval was an issue.

### Antecedent Conditions

Certain training experiences can have a dramatic effect on performer's self-esteem. For example, students who are the "stars" in a regional school often have a rude awakening when they suddenly become "one of the crowd" upon transferring to a more competitive arts program. This transition point usually happens in adolescence, away from home and in another state. Although no one is to blame, the student's response to these life events can result in deep-seated fears and insecurities.

Other performers may report a fateful audition that became a turning point in their lives. This was the case for one young dancer who wanted to quit performing.

## Case 6.0
## The Reluctant Student

I met with this 12-year-old dancer and her parents because of her disenchantment with ballet. On the one hand, this student worked extremely hard and was eager to take intensive private classes in order to progress. Yet she threatened to quit dancing whenever she was promoted to a more advanced level or had to audition for a summer course in a new school. Tears and tantrums would ensue for a couple of weeks until she settled into her dance classes with renewed enthusiasm. It was only after I questioned this dancer about her training that the source of her discomfort emerged. At the age of 11, this young girl had tried out for her first summer program. She was excited about attending the audition with her friends, and it was only when the letters of acceptance were handed out in public that she discovered she had not made the cut. Later successes had done little to alleviate her constant fear of rejection.

My goal in tailoring an intervention is to help performers achieve the best level of functioning within their particular range. Some performers may need help to manage the changes that occur during this career without becoming chronically overwhelmed by either positive or negative events. Other performers may require more of a balance between the way things are (realism) and the way they might be (idealism), while planning for inevitable events, such as aging, retirement, or making a career transition. It is important for performers to assume an active problem-solving approach toward necessary changes rather than avoiding responsibility or hoping for outside intervention.

As a psychologist who specializes in performance, I often help individuals discover new ways of coping with their perceived work problems. I may assist them in learning new skills to enhance their performance using a cognitive/behavioral approach or deal with more clinical issues, such as depression, eating disorders, or loss due to injury. A particular challenge is knowing how to handle the ethical dilemmas that often arise with elite performers, where unusual demands occur for the psychologist and patient alike.

## ETHICAL ISSUES IN THE CARE OF PERFORMERS

In the performing arts, with its focus on public display, success carries with it special perks, as well as the threat of exploitation. This situation can be especially problematic in psychotherapy. During treatment for personal problems, performers often request more time, attention, or latitude from therapists, who may be drawn into a valued team of "professional" friends. This leads to a number of ethical issues for the psychologist, particularly in terms of dual relationships.

Another concern involves the media, especially with high-profile entertainers. Whether it is a stay at the Betty Ford Clinic for substance abuse or revelations in group therapy, it is often difficult to maintain confidentiality. Let us consider the kinds of dilemmas that can come up when treating performers.

## The Performing Arts Community

Similar to any small community, performers are a close-knit group, where the majority lead essentially transparent lives—whether it is a faltering marriage, the death of a child, sexual preference, or their latest visit to the plastic surgeon. Among professionals, overlapping and dual relationships also abound: directors may act; dancers may direct; and therapists may perform as media psychologists or as performers themselves.

Similar to sports psychologists (Hays & Smith, 1996), performing arts psychologists are playing an increasingly active role in the lives of these professionals. The value of this approach is to be able finally to target work dysfunctions in a community where the level of stress is high and coping mechanisms are not always sufficient. The question is, to what degree does the treatment of celebrities result in substandard care?

## The Treatment of Celebrities

The medical profession was the first to address this issue at George Washington University in December 1990, after the treatment of celebrities was found to deviate from normal hospital routine. Problems involved premature discharges, deferred medical tests that might provoke embarrassment (e.g., a rectal exam), and competition between surgeons for the privilege of operating on a famous person. In terms of psychotherapy, the only definitive work has focused on instances of questionable behavior in Hollywood, where analysts occupied a prominent role in the movie industry (Farber & Green, 1993).

According to this source, it was not unusual for analysts to take their patients on vacations, request donations for research, and appear in their movies. Not surprisingly, this precedent also led to cases of malpractice. The irony is that analysts traditionally have advocated maintaining a formal distance between therapist and patient. Yet even Freud broke this rule; he was not above socializing with his favorite analysands or asking them for large donations. Princess Marie Bonaparte, a descendent of European royalty, is an example of a patient who also became a friend and helpmate, contributing vast sums of money to Freud's research and publishing ventures. Is this ethical behavior? For psychotherapists, there are few absolute rules.

## The Ethics Code

The American Psychological Association provides both mandatory obligations (e.g., no sexual intimacies with clients) and aspirations (e.g., maintain the highest standards of the profession) in its Ethics Code. Whereas there are few simple answers to an ethical dilemma, it is possible to work within a specified framework to promote appropriate decision making (Haas & Malouf, 1995).

Unfortunately, there are no specific guidelines that address the unique culture and social atmosphere of the performing arts. Practitioners are in even more unfamiliar territory when treating the famous performer who offers professional perks, such as choice social contacts. This is not standard fare for psychologists, unlike other successful practitioners. Although these situations do not lead inevitably to ethical violations, psychologists who work with performers need to be attuned to such issues as trust, social influence, and the development of dependency. Practitioners also require a thorough appreciation of the legal statutes in their state.

## Ethical Dilemmas

### The Structure of Psychotherapy

Is it therapy if it occurs in a dressing room, on tour, or during a rehearsal? For stars, such as Judy Garland, Marilyn Monroe, and Anne Bancroft, it was business as usual to have their therapists on the movie set during times of stress. This choice conflicts with an orthodox approach to treatment; however, APA's Ethics Code states that the structure of sessions depends on clinicians' discretion, as long as this occurs within their area of competence.

Practitioners also need to discuss how therapy will be carried out, including the nature and anticipated course of treatment, fees, and confidentiality. Past abuses with celebrity clients include scheduling excessive sessions, creating an unhealthy dependency, engendering exorbitant costs, and exposing the therapeutic relationship to a community plagued by gossip (Farber & Green, 1993).

An extreme example of an ethical violation occurred with one of the Beach Boys and a psychologist who used an unorthodox approach to wean him off drugs. Treatment involved round-the-clock therapy, where control was exerted over every aspect of the celebrity's life at the cost of $10,000 to $20,000 per month. This therapist also began acting as the singer's executive producer and business manager, co-wrote several songs with him, and claimed a 25% share of royalties. He lost his license, after being charged with causing severe emotional damage, psychological dependency, and financial exploitation of his patient.

A less extreme case is the unusual leeway given to O.J. Simpson, who was allowed to engage in mandatory therapy for spousal abuse *OVER* the phone. Although no one has made ethics charges, one might wonder if substandard care had been delivered in this case.

Less clear in terms of the therapy paradigm are phone sessions when performers are out on tour. For example, it is likely that if the therapist was called in to testify in court, state law would not consider telephone conversations to be privileged information, because this area is not well-defined.

APA also has yet to research whether a psychologist licensed in one state can actually provide services by phone in states where no license has been obtained. Although this is not considered to be a problem yet, APA will address complaints on a case-by-case basis. It is wise to inform clients who are using cell phones that conversations can be easily overheard. There is no legal recourse if this occurs, because this fact is considered to be common knowledge.

### Confidentiality: Maintenance and Limitations

According to a national survey, psychologists consider a breach in confidentiality to be the most serious ethical violation *AFTER* sexual misconduct (Haas, Malouf, & Mayerson, 1986). Yet confidentiality is often at stake if one presents a case involving a celebrity at conferences or refers to it among colleagues. One should either obtain informed consent or adequately disguise the information if it is to be used outside of therapy.

Importantly, this clause is still binding after the patient's death, making it unethical to speak about the performer posthumously without prior consent, unless it is to protect others from harm or under legal compulsion. The biography of the poet Ann Sexton is an example of an ethical violation, as this drew heavily on personal information and taped therapy sessions from her therapist after her suicide in 1974. A more recent instance involves the public statements made by Nicole Brown Simpson's therapist, who came forward after her murder.

The celebrity's estate can file ethics charges against the therapist under these circumstances. However, a legal suit, involving defamation of character, would be more difficult to pursue, as exposure is often an unavoidable aspect of life in the public eye (L. Haas, personal communication, April, 1995).

Likewise, it is important to discuss the limitations of confidentiality with celebrities early in treatment. Managed care, for example, represents an increasing intrusion into traditional practice arrangements. Many of my clients choose to pay out of pocket rather than have me submit personal information with insurance reports, where there is no guarantee of confidentiality.

Group therapy is also a difficult issue. Besides members of this community knowing each other, we have all heard stories of people who exploit celebrities' private revelations for personal gain. Adding an amendment to the therapy contract that stresses the importance of maintaining confidentiality can help, although the performer should know that the professional code of ethics applies *ONLY* to the psychologist—not to the other group members. Legal recourse, however, is a possibility.

Another potential problem involves referral sources, such as those from physicians, school officials and directors, because standards regarding confidentiality differ among professionals. I often have to consider how I want to share information without jeopardizing the person's privacy when a director sends a performer to see me and requests an update. Obtaining prior consent to discuss appropriate material can offset conflict to some degree.

### Dual Relationships

In the performing arts, there is also the potential to develop dual and multiple relationships. Therapists may see their clients at galas, in the studio, or at the theater. Whereas some of these meetings are unavoidable, therapists may want to discuss whether they will acknowledge their clients outside of the sessions. It is also important to refrain from taking on professional obligations if there is a preexisting relationship and it creates a risk of harm. Areas to avoid include collaborative work projects and ongoing social engagements, although this seems to be a common and fairly uncontested practice among psychiatrists in Hollywood.

If problems arise, the therapist must attempt to resolve them while keeping the best interests of the client in mind. Currently, complaints about nonsexual dual relationships comprise 7% of the American Psychological Association's alleged ethical violations (1997).

### Exploitative Relationships

It is wrong to exploit someone in an unequal relationship of power, but this standard also calls upon the sensitivity of therapists regarding their own needs for recognition and success. The successful performer is a powerful client who can generate important referrals. As a result, there is often a strong pull to satisfy the wishes of the client, as well as to advance one's own reputation through the media. Psychologists who use the professional relationship with the performer to enhance their self-esteem are making the welfare of the patient a lesser priority. Similarly, therapists should refrain from asking performers to use their connections to enhance their situation either personally or professionally.

What about the client who offers the therapist gifts or favors? Again, I handle these cases with care to avoid exploitation. Small tokens are rarely a problem, although it is important to consider the performer's motivation for offering them on a case-by-case basis. A large gift can have negative repercussions and may contaminate the goals of treatment. When in doubt, take a conservative approach, particularly when a solid professional identity in psychology hasn't been established yet.

Experience, however, does not necessarily rule out problems in this area. A lawsuit was filed against one of Chicago's most illustrious analysts in 1986 charging that he had brainwashed and overmedicated his patient into leaving the bulk of her $5 million estate to his psychiatric research institute, robbing her son of his inheritance (Farber & Green, 1993). The case was eventually settled out of court, and the analyst reportedly returned over $1 million. Although this is an extreme case, the therapeutic alliance is a significant factor when considering possible exploitation of the VIP.

### Conclusion

Fortunately, therapists can resolve many ethical issues before they become problems by discussing dilemmas with colleagues, by seeking out relevant reading material, and by keeping abreast of the legal statutes in their jurisdiction (Haas & Malouf, 1995). In making a decision, remember to distinguish between minimal requirements for ethically appropriate conduct and the ideals of psychology as a profession, because confusing the two can lead to paralysis and a pervasive sense of inadequacy. Although ethical alternatives cannot always be reduced to two choices— act or not act—therapists who are sensitive to issues concerning trust, social influence, and the development of dependency, can offset many ethical problems before they occur.

## FUTURE DIRECTIONS

 The emotional costs of a vocation in the performing arts can have a significant impact on the lives of dancers, musicians, actors and singers. Can students and professionals be better prepared to cope with the realities of this career? I believe that the answer is a resounding "yes" if we develop programs that use psychology as a guide in artistic development. Areas to target include training regimens, performance anxiety, eating disorders, injuries, unemployment, and retirement—all of which contribute to psychological dysfunction.

### Survival Skills

In order to thrive in what is, at best, a precarious situation, the aspiring performer must learn to handle the inevitable problems, disappointments, and losses that are likely to occur in addition to the joys and rewards. This process begins at the student level, as young performers confront personal limitations and are equalled or surpassed by others.

How can talented students be better prepared to cope with the realities of this profession? An antidote to the pernicious sense of insecurity that often accompanies young performers is building their self-esteem. Training programs that are designed to promote the emotional and physical well-being of students should be based on authentic feedback that is geared toward a problem-solving approach—not public humiliation! Teachers, who are often former performers, could also benefit from knowledge of child psychology.

In sports, Coach Effectiveness Training (CET) workshops offer behavioral guidelines for communicating effectively with young athletes, acquiring their respect, and relating with their parents (Smith & Smoll, 1990). These workshops also stress the importance of responding with sensitivity to individual differences, because all children are not equally talented. Research on five outcome variables, which include coaching behaviors, children's attitudes, self-esteem, performance anxiety, and attrition, support this training program's positive influence. A similar approach for teachers in the performing arts would also be helpful.

I believe that we can also alleviate performers' psychological problems through educational seminars that address the various stresses in this profession. I was delighted to learn that my old school, the High School of Performing Arts, which is now part of LaGuardia High School, has recently implemented a weekly course on "survival skills" for its arts students beginning with their freshman year.

Unfortunately, the biggest pitfall for aspiring performers—and one that is least likely to change—is unemployment. Students who must redefine career goals, due to lack of success or a serious injury, often require vocational counseling. These services are now available through several career transition centers to union members and/or non-members in the United States (e.g., Actors Work Program).

## Performing Arts Programs

Ideally, the optimal training program in the performing arts would prepare students in several art forms, as well as providing necessary skills for living, such as accounting and word processing. The International Organization for the Transition of Professional Dancers (IOTPD) is currently exploring this possibility on a global level. Established in 1993 in Lausanne, Switzerland, under the sponsorship of UNESCO, an agency of the United Nations, this non-profit group is developing guidelines to improve dancers' training and education, legal and social status, and support services, including psychological interventions.

In the United States, tentative steps are also being enacted to change the quality of college arts programs. A promising model is the one currently being carried out at Adelphi University in Garden City, New York, which involves a program of "cross-fertilization" in the arts. This model is based on a novel collaborative approach between the various departments of music, art and art history, communications, and the performing arts, with the goal of facilitating students' education and intellectual development.

To provide more time to acquire a well-rounded education, the college requirements for an arts major have been reduced from 93 credits to a more reasonable course load that ranges between 45 and 55 credits. Whether students take advantage of this opportunity will depend on how closely aligned these steps are with the basic needs of performers.

## Program Development

In order to work, programs for performers must cater to their specific needs, while building on the resources in this community. In addition to constructing ties with existing psychological services, programs must also exist that join together the performers, administrators, and artistic staff. A useful system for classifying preventive efforts, put forth by the Institute of Medicine's Committee on Prevention of Mental Disorders, makes several unique distinctions in program development (Mrazek & Haggerty, 1994). Programs may either be *universal* (i.e., focused on a whole population group), *selective* (i.e., targeted at high-risk individuals of the population), or *indicated* (e.g., geared toward high-risk individuals with small but detectable signs or symptoms of a disorder).

How would this work in the performing arts? One possibility for a universal program might be educational courses on injury prevention during training, alerting students about the potential traps of their specific art form and the benefits of engaging in healthy behaviors (e.g., good nutrition, stress-management, and sensible work habits). This program could also provide inservice training to residence hall personnel, teachers, and counselors. The cost per individual would be low with little risk from the intervention.

Selective interventions, on the other hand, could target subgroups of performers who are known to be at risk for certain problems (e.g., eating disorders in dancers or performance anxiety in musicians). These interventions do not need to exceed a moderate level of cost, and the programs should be based on known risk factors in order to devise effective selective interventions. For example, dancers most at risk for eating disorders appear to be those who are not naturally thin, have faulty notions surrounding weight loss, and/or have anatomical deficits that compromise their technique (Hamilton et al., 1997; Hamilton et al., 1988). An effective selective intervention would take these factors into consideration.

Lastly, indicated interventions would target performing arts students who manifest subclinical syndromes of mental disorders, such as depression, eating disorders, or performance anxiety. In these cases, the costs and risks would be weighed in terms of whether intervention would protect the individual from developing the disorder, keeping in mind that problems that have progressed to the clinical stage are more difficult to treat, treatment time takes longer, and the disorder is more likely to be accompanied by greater mental, physical, and occupational dysfunction.

## Training Regimens

It is important to educate the performing arts community to assume responsibility for ensuring the health and well-being of students during their training. Teaching children to perform—whether it is playing a musical instrument or executing ballet's technique—can easily take a decade, under the influence of an all-important teacher. Although few parents' consider training to be dangerous, some teachers may be abusive, publicly humiliating students or encouraging them to work with serious injuries. Under these circumstances, students suffer physically and emotionally; they experience more injuries, performance anxiety, self-sabotage, and thwarted career aspirations than those without this negative influence (Hamilton, 1997).

A recent article in *The New England Journal of Medicine* has called for an external agency to establish coaching standards and monitor the health and safety requirements for athletes (Tofler et al., 1996). There is a similar need for performers, which would narrow the gap between performing arts medicine and the community. This agency could be made up of specialists in the field—many of whom have a background as performers.

## Families of Performers

As a psychologist, I often feel caught in the middle between well-meaning parents who are overachievers and an overburdened child who has lost touch with his or her motivation. We could avoid the negative impact that some parents have on child performers by assisting them in making the performing arts a positive influence in their relationship with their child.

For example, many children's days are overscheduled with extra classes to improve their performance, robbing them of precious time to develop coping skills needed for life. Parents with an excessive focus on "winning" may also diminish the benefits of training, including their offspring's self-esteem, work ethic, self-discipline, and growing sense of mastery. Children who exhibit poor psychosocial adjustment warrant further attention, as there may be underlying problems.

Finally, we should encourage families to help their talented offspring develop lifelong habits that will be an asset outside of performing as well. It never hurts performers to explore other interests, get a well-rounded education, or practice time-management so that those interested in another career are able to do so. Training academies might also take a role in helping performers prepare for life off the stage through educational seminars and ties with career transition centers.

## Peak Performance

A big emphasis in sports, which could be incorporated into training programs, is mental skills training to improve performance using techniques such as visualization, goal-setting, and anxiety management. The goals of a mental skills training curriculum for performers include:

- grasping the "pressures" related to peak performance;
- controlling physical arousal, concentration, and attention;
- discussing strategies that create optimal performance; and
- acknowledging "paradoxes" in performing, such as how perfectionism often leads to stress and distraction.

To optimize performance, a training program should increase the person's knowledge of the specific mental skills that are useful in managing performance-related stressors at all levels. Of course, a key factor in ensuring program effectiveness is adherence, which depends on several personal and situational variables in sports (Bull, 1991). For example, mental skills training works best if it is individualized, integrated into physical practice sessions, and updated regularly to allow for individual changes over time.

## Performance Psychology

Performance is a growing preoccupation in today's society, whether it is riding the stockmarket or creating the next jingle in a competitive advertising marketplace. In fact, many clients in the workforce struggle with psychological problems associated with the pressure to advance, to be flawless, or to bring into existence a new and improved rendition. All professionals share concerns about their performance; the difference is that certain careers may emphasize one component over another.

For example, although success in sports and dance is based on physical skill, athletes focus primarily on winning, whereas performers generally compete with themselves in the quest for perfection. Likewise, the need to be creative is paramount in professions such as a playwright, and to a much lesser extent in interpretive athletes or artists. All may suffer from performance anxiety; however, the processes that produce this effect will differ, depending on the interaction between the person and the environment.

On the positive side, a mindset focused on achievement can lead to a sense of mastery and self-esteem, as well as secondary benefits to society as a whole. The risk occurs when one's pursuit of peak performance occurs at any cost, the most glaring example of which is the death of seven-year-old Jessica Dubroff during her failed cross-country airplane trip last year.

Currently, third-party payers and consumers increasingly require specialists from doctoral and postdoctoral programs. This necessity may significantly affect psychologists' accreditation, education, training, practice, and professional identities in the future. As advances continue in our theoretical and empirical knowledge of performance psychology, I believe that we will increasingly apply this information to select problems and populations in particular settings.

This emphasis on performance could eventually lead to a comprehensive psychology that cuts across different domains, such as clinical, media, sports, and the arts. Perhaps, the time has come for formal training programs that offer a proficiency in performance psychology through workshops and continuing education courses, with special attention to the unique stresses in the performing arts.

# Appendix
## An Overview
## Of Narcissism

I t is an understatement to say that numerous articles, essays, and books have been written on narcissism both as a personality trait and as a pathological entity. I invite the reader who wants to know more about the salient features of the topic to review this modest summary.

### NARCISSISM: A DIMENSION OF PERSONALITY

Until recent times, narcissism has been a term used in psychoanalytic circles to describe certain aspects of personality development. As such it has been based on theory rather than on empirical evidence, where it served primarily as a metaphor rather than an empirically based descriptor of human behavior.

In the last decade, this personality dynamic has been thrust into our understanding of human behavior, with the American Psychiatric Association's delineation of the diagnostic criteria for the *narcissistic personality disorder* in the DSM-III (APA, 1980), DSM-III-R (APA, 1987), and DSM-IV (APA, 1994).[1] The behavioral definition of this disorder is made up of eight characteristic traits that, when exhibited in their extreme form, constitute the syndrome. Still, it is important to distinguish among the terms "normal" narcissism, pathological narcissism, and narcissistic personality disorder in order to be conceptually and technically precise (Auerbach, 1984; Emmons, 1987; Solomon, 1985; Watson et al., 1995).

- *Normal narcissism* is considered to be an attribute of all personality functioning (Freud, 1914/1957) and refers to those parts involving: (a) self-representation, (b) self-focus and self-investment, (c) self-esteem regulation and (d) certain aspects of object relations (Duruz, 1981; Pulver, 1970; Stolorow, 1975). It involves a realistic self-image, based on the combination of good and bad aspects of the self. Thus, normal narcissism involves healthy, positive self-esteem; self-concept; self-feeling; or self-regard.

- *Pathological narcissism* involves a disruption of the four psychological aspects involved in narcissism, making it a feature of all psychopathology (Kernberg, 1975). Good and bad images of the self are split off rather than integrated, which result in extreme fluctuations in self-concept: "egocentricism and low self-esteem, omnipotence and helplessness, over-control and weak identity" (Kreuger, 1976).

- *The narcissistic personality disorder* is a specific psychological entity, defined theoretically by the presence of certain characteristic disturbances of narcissistic and other personality processes and empirically by the presence of a set of specific character traits. Symptoms in the recent version of the DSM-IV include: grandiosity, a need for admiration, preoccupation with idealized fantasies, and severe disturbances in personal relationships.

## NARCISSISM IN THE PERFORMING ARTIST

### Self-Psychology

Kohut's formulations regarding the development of the "self" speak directly to the exhibitionistic and aesthetic components that are the essence of a performing art. In addition, this approach accounts for the healthy aspects seen in performing artists, by encompassing within a theory of personality development, the benefits derived from artistic pursuits.

In order to test this premise empirically, we surveyed 100 women in four careers which differed in personal display (high/low)—defined by how much they exposed themselves to an audience—and aesthetic ideals (artist/nonartist), with a control group of traditional women, using measures of healthy and pathological narcissism and personal adjustment (Hamilton, 1988a). To date, this is the only study that has directly evaluated the role of narcissism in performers.

Women who have been classified as being in high display groups (ballet dancers and bankers who present before board meetings) had significantly more healthy narcissism (65% vs 40%, p<.007) compared to those in work with low display (orchestral musicians and nurses). Furthermore, the type of profession was related to pathological narcissism. Compared to nonartists, performers had more pathology, falling closely (within one standard deviation) to patients diagnosed with a narcissistic personality disorder. And yet performers' personal adjustment was *not* compromised, as measured by the difference between these women's real and ideal self evaluations, underscoring the role narcissism can play in mediating both health and pathology in performing artists—a fact that has not been addressed in previous studies. In addition, these results tell us that the arts may have therapeutic value, as several theories suggest, given the performer's adequate personal adjustment in relation to other professional women.

## ART AS THERAPY

Kohut (1977) explored the therapeutic aspects of artistic pursuits in his work with highly disturbed patients whom he frequently classified as having a narcissistic personality disorder. Viewed as a structure-building phenomenon, he believed that creativity could result in increased self-cohesion and a rearrangement of the narcissistic sector of the personality. For this reason, he saw the emergence of artistic pursuits as an indicator of improved psychological functioning, even in the case of severe narcissistic disturbances.

Kohut advised going into psychoanalytic treatment to establish an area within the self that directs the flow of narcissistic strivings toward creative expression, which might even cure the disorder. He stated:

> In many instances, the reshaping of the narcissistic structures and their integration into the personality must be rated as a more genuine and valid result of therapy than the patient's precarious compliance with demands for a change of his narcissism into object love. (Kohut, 1971, p.270)

Therefore, he saw artistic pursuits in highly disturbed patients as a sign that narcissistic equilibrium was being attained through the development and integration of structures within the individual's personality.

## KOHUT'S THEORY OF HEALTHY NARCISSISM

In essence, the main thrust of Kohut's position is that there is a separate narcissistic line of development, which is never outgrown but is transformed into a bipolar self, based on healthy ambitions and strongly held ideals and values. These poles are derived from early relational configurations, where "mirroring" self-objects were needed to reflect the infant's evolving grandiosity and "idealized" self-objects that permitted fusion with an omnipotent and all-perfect other.

In optimal development, Kohut believed that these poles gradually become internalized into a permanent psychic structure that represents the "true" self and forms the basis of self-love and healthy narcissism. In addition, because this line continues to undergo progressive transformations, there is the capacity for further development. Thus, the need for the type of narcissistic gratification that comes from objects and pursuits that reflect the self continues throughout the person's lifetime (Kohut, 1977).

In the performing arts, this developmental sequence of encompassing mirroring and idealized self-objects is a natural phenomenon because the artist's grandiosity and exhibitionism are essential ingredients in any production. By displaying the seeming perfection of the "self" before an admiring audience, performers seek confirmation of their own uniqueness. This experience duplicates the early mirroring experience and presents an opportunity for talented professionals to cater directly to the narcissistic part of their personality. Additionally, there is a strong tendency for artists to revere the aesthetic values upon which their art form is based. As a result, these aesthetic standards are frequently treated as idealized self-objects with which the artist seeks to identify and merge. Finally, in order to mediate between their exhibitionistic strivings on the one hand, and a set of internalized ideals on the other, performers must have sufficient ego strength to undergo many years of training.

## Conclusion

The above synopsis highlights the continuum between health and pathology, forming the basis for narcissism's role in the performing arts, which offers both advantages and liabilities on those who aspire to its aesthetic ideals. At its best, performers' self-esteem is enhanced when their efforts culminate in mastery, direction, and professional recognition from others.

## NOTE

[1]Although the creators of DSM nosology have been criticized as tacitly reifying personality disorders, the general consensus is that these typologies restore the unity of personality by integrating seemingly diverse elements into a single coordinated syndrome (Millon, 1994).

# RESOURCE DIRECTORY

This section provides contact information for a select group of performing arts medicine organizations, periodicals, and related services that may be useful resources for performers, teachers, and health care practitioners.

## CAREER TRANSITION CENTERS

**Actors' Work Program**
165 West 46th Street
New York, NY 10036
(212) 840-3401.

5757 Wilshire Boulevard, 9th floor
Los Angeles, CA 90036
(213) 939-1801.

**Career Transition for Dancers** (CTFD)
1727 Broadway, 2nd floor
New York, NY 10019
(212) 581-7043.

5757 Wilshire Blvd, 8th floor
Los Angeles, CA 90036
(213) 549-6660.

**CareerLine** (CTFD)
national "hotline"
(800) 581-2833 outside of
(718) and (212) area codes.

**Dancer Transition Resource Centre**
66 Gerrard Street E, Suite 202
Toronto, Canada M5B 1G3
(416) 595-5655.

## HEALTH INSURANCE

### Dance Professionals Associates (DPA)
440 East 81th Street, Suite 6G
New York, NY 10028
(212) 535-3757
(888) DPA-3560

## PERFORMING ARTS MEDICINE CLINICS

The following clinics and referral networks offer a variety of services and fee scales
to performers.

### The Artists Health Centre Project
c/o Joysanne Sidimus
66 Gerrard Street E, Suite 202
Toronto, Canada M5B 1G3
(416) 595-5655.

### British Performing Arts Medical Trust
18 Ogle Street
London, England
W1P 7LG
44-171-636-6860.

### Performing Artists Program
Section of Physical Medicine & Rehabiltation
Virginia Mason Medical Center
1100 Ninth Avenue
P.O. Box 900
Seattle, WA 98111
(206) 223-6600.

### Dance Medicine Australia
c/o 10 Cacio Place
Prahran, Victoria
Australia
61 39 525 1566.

**Dept. of Physical Medicine & Rehabilitation**
Loma Linda University Medical Center
11234 Anderson Street
Loma Linda, CA 92354
(909) 796-3741.

**Division of Performing Arts Medicine**
Evan Brook Orthopaedic & Sports Medicine Associates, Ltd.
1144 Wilmette Avenue
Wilmette, IL 60091
(847) 853-9400.

**Harkness Center for Dance Injuries**
Hospital for Joint Diseases
301 East 17th Street
New York, NY 10003
(212) 598-6022.

**Health Program for Performing Artists**
San Francisco Medical Center
University of California
400 Parnassus Avenue, 5th floor
San Francisco, CA 94143
(415) 476-3452.

**Rusk Institute of Rehabiltation Medicine**
NYU School of Medicine
400 East 34th Street
New York, NY 10016
(212) 263-7300.

**Kenny Rehabilitation Associates**
Sister Kenny Institute
800 E. 28th Street
Minneapolis, MN 55407
(612) 863-4495.

**Mayo Clinic**
200 First Street, SW
Rochester, MN 55905
(507) 284-2511 X7129.

## Medical Program for the Performing Arts
Jewish Hospital
216 S. Kingshighway
St. Louis, MO 63108
(314) 454-STAR.

## Medical Program for Performing Artists
Rehabilitation Institute of Chicago
345 E. Superior Street
Chicago, IL 60611
(312) 908-ARTS.

## Miller Institute for Performing Artists
St. Luke's-Roosevelt Hospital
425 West 59th Street, 6th floor
New York, NY 10019
(212) 523-6200.

## National Rehabilitation Hospital
3 Bethesda Metro Center, Suite 950
Bethesda, MD 20814
(301) 654-9160.

## Neurologic Rehabilitation Unit
Bethesda Hospital
3655 Vista Avenue
St. Louis, MO 63110
(314) 772-9200.

## Performing Artists' Health Program
Centre for Human Performance & Health Promotion
Sir William Osler Health Institute
565 Sanatorium Road, Suite 205
Hamilton, Ontario L9C 7N4
(905) 574-5444.

## Musicians Clinic
340 College Street, Suite 440
Toronto, Ontario M5T 349
(416) 966-8742.

**Performing Arts Medicine**
Kaiser Permanente
7601 Stoneridge Drive
Pleasanton, CA 94588
(510) 847-5000.

**Performing Arts Clinic** (Neurology Dept.)
Brigham & Women's Hospital
45 Francis Street
Boston, MA 02115
(617) 732-5771.

**Performing Arts Medicine Program**
Indiana University School of Medicine
541 Clinical Drive
Indianapolis, IN 46202
(317) 274-4225.

**Rebound Sports Medicine** (Eastside location)
857 Auto Mall Road
Bloomington, IN 47401
(812) 332-6200.

**Rebound Sports Medicine** (Westside location)
639 S. Walker, Suite B
Bloomington, IN 47403
(812) 336-9333.

**St. Joseph's Occupational Health Center**
3413 W. Pacific Avenue, Suite 204 (Hand therapy)
Burbank, CA 91505
(818) 953-4430.

**The Southwest Regional Arts Medicine Center**
The Institute of Rehabilitation & Research
Texas Medical Center
1333 Moursund Avenue
Houston, TX 77030-3405
(713) 799-5000

**University of Colorado Health Sciences Center**
Department of Neurology
Campus Box B 183
4200 E. Ninth Avenue
Denver, CO 80262
(303) 315-7517.

## JOURNALS & TEXTBOOKS

*International Journal of Arts Medicine*
MMB Music, Inc.
3526 Washington Avenue
St. Louis, MO 63103
(314) 531-9635.

*Journal of Dance Medicine & Science*
J. Michael Ryan Publishing, Inc.
24 Crescent Drive North
Andover, NJ 07821-4000
(201) 786-7777.

*Medicine des Arts*
Alexitere Publishing
715 chemin du Quart
82000 Montauban, France
33-5-63-202090.

*Medical Problems of Performing Artists*
Hanley & Belfus, Inc.
210 S. 13th Street
Philadelphia, PA 19107
(215) 546-4995
(800) 962-1892.

*Textbook of Performing Arts Medicine* (1991)
(EDs) R.T. Sataloff, A.G. Brandfonbrener, &
R.J. Lederman; New York: Raven Press.
800-777-2295
ISBN 0-88167-698-5

# PROFESSIONAL ASSOCIATIONS

**Arts Anonymous**
World Service
Ansonia Station
P.O. Box 175
New York, NY 10023
(212) 873-7075.

**International Arts Medicine Association**
3600 Market Street
Philadelphia, PA 19104
(610) 525-3784.

**International Association for Dance
Medicine and Science**
c/o Jan Dunn, President
2555 Andrew Drive
Superior, CO 80027
(303) 494-9450.

**Performing Arts Medicine Association**
c/o Ralf Manchester, M.D., S.C., Treasurer
250 Crittenden Boulevard
Box 617
Rochester, NY 14642
(716) 275-2679.

**Psychology & the Arts**
Division 10 Administrative Office
American Psychological Association
750 First Street, N.E.
Washington D.C. 20002-4242
(202) 336-6013.

**American Association for
Psychology and the Arts**
c/o Sherrie Raz, M.S., Pres.
430 Clematis Street
West Palm Beach, FL 33401
(516) 852-6868
(954) 755-8247

# REFERENCES

Amabile, T. M. (1990). Within you, without you: The social psychology of creativity, and beyond. In M. A. Runco & R. S. Albert (Eds.), *Theories of creativity* (pp. 61-91). Newbury Park, CA: Sage.

Ambrose, D., Allen, J., & Huntley, S. (1994). Mentorship of the highly creative. *Roeper Review, 17*(2), 131-134.

American Psychiatric Association (1980). *Diagnostic and statistical manual of mental disorders* (3rd ed.). Washington, DC: Author.

American Psychiatric Association (1987). *Diagnostic and statistical manual of mental disorders* (Rev. 3rd ed.). Washington, DC: Author.

American Psychiatric Association (1994). *Diagnostic and statistical manual of mental disorders* (4th ed.). Washington, DC: Author.

American Psychological Association (1997). Report of the ethics committee, 1996. *American Psychologist, 52*, 875-905.

Ashby, H. U., Lee, R. R., & Duke, E. H. (1979, September). *A narcissistic personality disorder MMPI scale.* Paper presented at the annual meeting of the American Psychological Association, New York.

Attie, I., & Brooks-Gunn, J. (1989). Development of eating problems in adolescent girls: A longitudinal study. *Developmental Psychology, 25*, 70-79.

Attie, I., Brooks-Gunn, J., & Petersen, A. C. (1987). A developmental perspective on eating disorders and eating problems. In M. Lewis & S. M. Miller (Eds.), *Handbook of developmental psychopathology* (pp. 409-420). New York: Plenum Press.

Auerbach, J. S. (1984). Validation of two scales for Narcissistic Personality Disorder. *Journal of Personality Assessment, 48*, 649-653.

Azar, B. (1995). Social-phobia treatments may also work for problem shyness. *APA Monitor, 26*(11), 24.

Barlow, D. H., & Liebowitz, M. R. (1995). Specific phobia and social phobia. In H. I. Kaplan & B. J. Sadock (Eds.), *Comprehensive textbook of psychiatry/VI* (Vol 1, pp. 1204-1218). Baltimore, MD: Williams & Wilkins.

Beaumont, P. J. V., Russell, J. D., & Touyz, S. W. (1993). Treatment of anorexia nervosa. *Lancet, 341*, 1635-1640.

Bennett, W., & Gurin, J. (1982). *The dieter's dilemma.* New York: Basic Books, Inc.

Berman, C., & McCormick, P. (1993, January). When one child is a star. *Parents Magazine, 68*, 68.

Bers, S. A. (1988, April). *Self-devaluation in the disturbed sense of self of anorexia nervosa patients.* Paper presented at the Third International Conference of Eating Disorders, New York.

Bion, W. R. (1959). *Experiences in groups.* New York: Basic Books.

Blackburn, G. L., Wilson, G. T., Kanders, B. S., Stein, L. J., Lavin, P. T., Adler, J., & Brownell, K. D. (1989). Weight cycling: The experience of human dieters. *American Journal of Clinical Nutrition, 49*(suppl. 1), 1105-1109.

Bleiberg, E. (1994). Normal and pathological narcissism in adolescence. *American Journal of Psychotherapy, 48*(1), 30-51.

Bowlby, J. (1973). *Attachment and loss: Vol. 2: Separation, anxiety, and anger.* New York: Basic Books.

Bradshaw, J. (1988). *The Family: A revolutionary way of self-discovery.* Pompano Beach, FL: Health Communications.

Brandfonbrener, A. G. (1991). Epidemiology of the medical problems of performing artists. In R. T. Sataloff, A. G. Brandfonbrener, & R. J. Lederman (Eds.), *Textbook of performing arts medicine* (pp. 25-69). New York: Raven.

Brant, M. (1995, October 23). Pumping irony: Thin meets gym. *Newsweek, 126*, 88.

Brockner, J., & Hulton, A. J. B. (1978). How to reverse the vicious cycle of low self-esteem. The importance of attentional focus. *Journal of Experimental Social Psychology, 14*, 564-578.

Bruch, H. (1973). *Eating Disorders: Obesity, anorexia nervosa, and the person within.* New York: Basic Books.

Brustad, R. J. (1988). Affective outcomes in competitive youth sport: The influence of intrapersonal and socialization factors. *Journal of Sport & Exercise Psychology, 10*, 307-321.

Bull, S. J. (1991). Personal and situational influences on adherence to mental skills training. *Journal of Sport & Exercise Psychology, 13*, 121-132.

Buri, J. R., Murphy, P., Richtsmeier, L. M., & Komar, K. K. (1992). Stability of parental nurturance as a salient predictor of self-esteem. *Psychological Reports, 71*, 535-543.

Burke, R. J., & Kirchmeyer, C. (1990). Initial career orientations, stress, and burnout in policeworkers. *Canadian Police College Journal, 14*, 28-36.

Burns, D. D. (1980). *Feeling good: The new mood therapy.* New York: Morrow.

Bushnell, J. A., Wells, J. E., Hornblow, A. R., Oakley-Browne, M. A., & Joyce, P. (1990). Prevalence of three bulimia syndromes in the general population. *Psychological Medicine, 20*, 671-680.

Butler, C. (1995). Investigating the effects of stress on the success and failure of music conservatory students. *Medical Problems of Performing Artists, 10*, 24-31.

Cannon, W. B. (1929). *Bodily changes in pain, hunger, fear and rage* (2nd ed). NY: D Appleton Century Co.

Cash, T. F., & Horton, C. E. (1983). Aesthetic surgery: Effects of rhinoplasty on the social perception of patients by others. *Plastic and Reconstructive Surgery, 72*, 543-548.

Clark, D. B. (1989). Performance-related medical and psychological disorders in instrumental musicians. *Annals of Behavioral Medicine, 11*, 28-34.

Clark, D. B., & Agras, W. S. (1991). The assessment and treatment of performance anxiety in musicians. *American Journal of Psychiatry, 148,* 598-605.

Colangelo, N., & Dettman, D. F. (1983). A review of research on parents and families of gifted children. *Exceptional Children, 50*(1), 20-27.

Cooper, E. (1986). *The sexual perspective: Homosexuality and art in the last 100 years in the west.* London: Routledge & Kegan Paul Ltd.

Csikszentmihalyi, M. (1990). *Flow: The psychology of optimal experience.* New York: Harper & Row.

Csikszentmihalyi, M., Rathunde, K., & Whalen, S. (1993). *Talented teenagers: The roots of success and failure.* Cambridge: Cambridge University Press.

Curtis, J. M., & Cowell, D. R. (1993). Relation of birth order and scores on measures of pathological narcissism. *Psychological Reports, 72,* 311-315.

Davis, C. (1990). Body image and weight preoccupation: A comparison between exercising and non-exercising women. *Appetite, 15,* 13-21.

Demb, J. (1992). Are gay men artistic? A review of the literature. *Journal of Homosexuality, 23*(4), 83-92.

Donaldson-Pressman, S., & Pressman, R. M. (1994). *The narcissistic family: Diagnosis and treatment.* New York: Lexington Books.

Dudek, S. Z., Berneche, R., Berube, H., & Royer, S. (1991). Personality determinants of the commitment to the profession of art. *Creativity Research Journal, 4,* 367-389.

Duffy, M. (1991, May 6). Why golden voices fade. *Time, 137,* 74-75.

Dunning, J. (1985). *But first a school: The first fifty years of the School of American Ballet.* New York: Viking Press.

Duruz, N. (1981). The psychoanalytic concept of narcissism. *Psychoanalysis and Contemporary Thought, 4,* 3-67.

Dweck, C. S. (1995, September). Students' theories about their intelligence: Implications for the gifted. Paper presented at the Fifth Annual Esther Katz Rosen Symposium on the Psychological Development of Gifted Children, Lawrence, Kansas.

Eagles, J. M., Johnston, M. I., Hunter, D., Lobban, M., & Millar, H. R. (1995). Increasing incidence of anorexia nervosa in the female population of Northeast Scotland. *American Journal of Psychiatry, 152,* 1266-1271.

Eisler, R. M., Skidmore, J. R., & Ward, C. H. (1988). Masculine gender-role stress: Predictor of anger, anxiety, and health-risk behaviors. *Journal of Personality Assessment, 52,* 133-141.

Emmons, R. A. (1987). Narcissism: Theory and measurement. *Journal of Personality and Social Psychology, 52,* 11-17.

Farber, S., & Green, M. (1993). *Hollywood on the couch: A candid look at the overheated love affair between psychiatrists and movie makers.* New York: William Morrow & Co.

Fava, G. A., Grandi, S., Canestrari, R., & Molnar, G. (1990). Prodromal symptoms in primary major depressive disorder. *Journal of Affective Disorders, 19,* 149-152.

Fishbein, M., Middlestadt, S. E., Ottati, V., Straus, S., & Ellis, A. (1988). Medical problems among ICSOM musicians: Overview of a national survey. *Medical Problems in Performing Artists, 3,* 1-14.

Fisher, A. C., Domm, M. A., & Wuest, D. A. (1988). Adherence to sports-injury rehabilitation programs. *Physician and Sportsmedicine, 16*(7), 47-52.

Flaherty, L. T. (1982). To love and/or work: The ideological dilemma of young women. *Adolescent Psychiatry, 10,* 41-51.

Fordyce, W. E. (1981). Behavioral methods in medical rehabilitation. *Neuroscience and Behavioral Reviews, 5,* 391-396.

Forsyth, S., & Kolenda, P. M. (1966). Competition, cooperation, and group cohesion in the ballet company. *Psychiatry 29,* 123-145.

Freeman, J. (1979). *Gifted children: Their identification and development in a social context* Lancaster, PA: MTP.

Freiberg, P. (1995). Creativity is influenced by our social networks. *The APA Monitor, 26*(8), p. 21.

Freud, S. (1914/1957). On narcissism: An introduction. In J. Strachey (Ed. and Trans.), *The standard edition of the complete psychological works of Sigmund Freud* (Vol. 14, pp. 67-102). London: Hogarth.

Freud, S. (1963). Introductory lectures on psycho-analysis (Parts I an II, 1915-1916). *The standard edition of the complete psychological works of Sigmund Freud,* (Vol. 15). London: Hogarth.

Fyer, A. J., Mannuzza, S., Chapman, T. F., Liebowitz, M. R., & Klein, D. F. (1993). A direct interview family study of social phobia. *Archives of General Psychiatry, 50,* 286-293.

Gabbard, G. O. (1983). Further contributions to the understanding of stage fright: Narcissistic issues. *Journal of the American Psychoanalytic Association, 31,* 423-441.

Gardner, H. (1993). *Multiple intelligences: The theory in practice.* New York: Basic Books.

Garner, D. M. (1993). Pathogenesis of anorexia nervosa. *Lancet, 341,* 1631-1635.

Garner, D. M., & Garfinkel, P. E. (1979). The eating attitudes test: An index of the symptoms of anorexia nervosa. *Psychological Medicine, 9,* 273-279.

Garner, D. M., & Garfinkel, P. E. (1980). Socio-cultural factors in the development of anorexia nervosa. *Psychological Medicine, 10,* 647-656.

Garner, D. M., Garfinkel, P. E., Rockert, W., & Olmsted, M. P. (1987). A prospective study of eating disturbances in the ballet. *Psychotherapy and Psychosomatics, 48,* 170-175.

Garner, D. M., Garfinkel, P. E., Schwartz, D., & Thompson, M. (1980). Cultural expectations of thinness in women. *Psychological Reports, 47,* 483-491.

Garner, D. M., Olmsted, M. P., & Garfinkel, P. E. (1983). Does anorexia nervosa occur on a continuum? Subgroups of weight-preoccupied women and their relationship to anorexia nervosa. *International Journal of Eating Disorders, 2*(4), 11-20.

Garner, D. M., Rockert, W., Olmsted, M. P., Johnson, C., & Coscina, D. V. (1985). Psychoeducational principles in the treatment of bulimia and anorexia nervosa. In D. M. Garner & P. E. Garfinkel, *Handbook of psychotherapy for anorexia nervosa and bulimia* (pp. 513-572). New York: Guilford Press.

Gates, G. A., Saegert, J., Wilson, N., Johnson, L., Shepherd, A., & Hearne III, E. M. (1985). Effect of B blockade on singing performance. *Annals of Otology, Rhinology and Laryngology, 94,* 570-574.

Geist, R. A. (1985). Therapeutic dilemmas in the treatment of anorexia nervosa: A self-psychological perspective. In S. W. Emmett (Ed.), *Theory and treatment of anorexia nervosa and bulimia: Biomedical, sociocultural, and psychological perspectives* (pp. 268-288). New York: Brunner/Mazel.

Goertzel, M. G., Goertzel, V., & Goertzel, T. G. (1978). *300 eminent personalities.* San Francisco: Jossey-Bass.

Goin, J. M., & Goin, M. K. (1981). *Changing the body: Psychological effects of plastic surgery.* Baltimore, MD: Williams & Wilkins.

Goleman, D. (1991, October 15). Happy or sad, a mood can prove contagious. *The New York Times*, pp. C1, C8.

Golembiewski, R. T., & Kim, B. (1989). Self-esteem and phases of burnout. *Organization Development Journal, 7*, 51-58.

Goodsitt, A. (1977). Narcissistic disturbances in anorexia nervosa. In S. C. Feinstein & P. L. Giovacchini (Eds.), *Adolescent psychiatry* (Vol. 5, pp. 304-312). New York: Jason Aronson.

Goodsitt, A. (1983). Self-regulatory disturbances in eating disorders. *International Journal of Eating Disorders, 2*(3), 51-60.

Goodsitt, A. (1985). Self psychology and the treatment of anorexia nervosa. In D. M. Garner & P. E. Garfinkel (Eds.), *Handbook of psychotherapy for anorexia nervosa and bulimia* (pp. 55-82). New York: Guilford Press.

Gough H. G., & Heilbrun, Jr., A. B. (1983). *The adjective checklist.* Palo Alto, CA: Consulting Psychologists, Press, Inc.

Gould, D., Feltz, D., & Weiss, M. (1985). Motives of participating in competitive youth swimming. *International Journal of Sport Psychology, 16*, 126-140.

Green, R., & Money, J. (1966). Stage-acting, role-taking, and effeminate impersonation during boyhood. *Archives of General Psychiatry, 15*, 535-538.

Haas, L. J., & Malouf, J. L. (1995). *Keeping up the good work: A practitioner's guide to mental health ethics* (2nd ed.). Sarasota, FL: Professional Resource Press.

Haas, L. J., Malouf, J. L., & Mayerson, N. H. (1986). Ethical dilemmas in psychological practice: Results of a national survey. *Professional Psychology: Research and Practice, 17*, 316-321.

Hamann, D. L. (1982). An assessment of anxiety in instrumental and vocal performances. *Journal of Research in Music Education, 30*, 77-90.

Hamann, D. L., & Sobaje, M. (1983). Anxiety and the college musician: A study of performance conditions and subject variables. *Psychology of Music, 11*, 37-50.

Hamilton, L. H. (1988a). In pursuit of the ideal: Narcissism and the performing artist. (Doctoral dissertation, Adelphi University, 1989.) *Dissertation Abstracts International,* AGG8814624.

Hamilton, L. H. (1988b, April). The Relationship between Pathological Narcissism and Eating Problems in Professional Women. Paper presented at the Third International Conference on Eating Disorders, New York.

Hamilton, L. H. (1995, December). Sexual harassment: What is happening in our dance schools? *Dance Magazine*, 86-88.

Hamilton, L. H. (1996, November). Dancers' health survey, part I. To your health. *Dance Magazine*, 56-60.

Hamilton, L. H. (1997, February). Dancers' health survey, part II. From injury to peak performance. *Dance Magazine*, 60-65.

Hamilton, L. H. (1997). A psychological approach to the rehabilitation of injured performers. *Orthopedic Physical Therapy Clinics of North America 6*(2), 131-143.

Hamilton, L. H., Brooks-Gunn, J., & Warren, M. P. (1985). Sociocultural influences on eating disorders in professional female ballet dancers. *International Journal of Eating Disorders, 4*, 465-477.

Hamilton, L. H., Brooks-Gunn, J., & Warren, M. P. (1986). Nutritional intake of female dancers: A reflection of eating problems. *International Journal of Eating Disorders, 5*, 925-934.

Hamilton, L. H., Brooks-Gunn, J., Warren, M. P., & Hamilton, W. G. (1987). The impact of thinness and dieting on the professional ballet dancer. *Medical Problems of Performing Artists, 2*, 117-122.

Hamilton, L. H., Brooks-Gunn, J., Warren, M. P., & Hamilton, W. G. (1988). The role of selectivity in the pathogenesis of eating problems in ballet dancers. *Medicine and Science in Sports and Exercise, 20*, 560-565.

Hamilton, L. H., & Hamilton, W. G. (1991). Classical ballet: Balancing the costs of artistry and athleticism. *Medical Problems of Performing Artists, 6*, 39-44.

Hamilton, L. H., & Hamilton, W. G. (1994). Occupational stress in classical ballet: The impact in different cultures. *Medical Problems of Performing Artists, 9*, 35-38.

Hamilton, L. H., Hamilton, W. G., Meltzer, J. D., Marshall, P., & Molnar, M. (1989). Personality, stress, and injuries in professional ballet dancers. *The American Journal of Sports Medicine, 17*, 263-267.

Hamilton, L. H., Hamilton, W. G., Warren, M. P., Keller, K., & Molnar, M. (1997). Factors contributing to the attrition rate in elite ballet students. *Journal of Dance Medicine & Science, 1*, 131-138.

Hamilton, L. H., & Kella, J. J. (1992, May). Personality profile of professional musicians. Paper presented at the conference on Advances in Performing Arts Medicine II, New York.

Hamilton, L. H., Kella, J. J., & Hamilton, W. G. (1995). Personality and occupational stress in elite performers. *Medical Problems of Performing Artists, 10*, 86-89.

Hamilton, L. H., Stricker, G., & Josephs, L. (1991). The organizational aspects of classical ballet: Transference and the role of the leader. *Medical Problems of Performing Artists, 6*, 78-83.

Hamilton, W. G., Geppert, M. J., & Thompson, F. M. (1996). Pain in the posterior aspect of the ankle in dancers: Differential diagnosis and operative treatment. *Journal of Bone and Joint Surgery, 78-A*, 1491-1500.

Harman, S. E. (1991). The evolution of performing arts medicine as seen through the literature. In R. T. Sataloff, A. G. Brandfonbrener, & R. J. Lederman (Eds.), *Textbook of performing arts medicine* (pp. 1-24). New York: Raven.

Hays, K. F., & Smith, R. J. (1996). Incorporating sport and exercise psychology into clinical practice. In J. L. Van Raalte & B. W. Brewer (Eds.), *Exploring sport and exercise psychology* (pp. 413-429).

Helson, R. (1990). Creativity in women: Outer and inner views over time. In M. A. Runco & R. S. Albert (Eds.), *Theories of creativity* (pp. 46-58). Newbury Park, CA: Sage.

Hoek, H. W. (1993). Review of the epidemiological studies of eating disorders. *International Review of Psychiatry, 5*, 61-74.

Janos, P. M., Fung, H. C., & Robinson, N. M. (1985). Self-concept, self-esteem, and peer relations among gifted children who feel "different." *Gifted Child Quarterly, 29*, 78-82.

Janos, P. M., & Robinson, N. M. (1985). Psychosocial development in intellectually gifted children. In F. D. Horowitz & M. O'Brien (Eds.), *The gifted and talented: Developmental perspectives* (pp. 149-195). Washington, DC: American Psychological Association.

John, O. P., & Robins, R. W. (1994). Accuracy and bias in self-perception: Individual differences in self-enhancement and the role of narcissism. *Journal of Personality and Social Psychology, 66,* 206-219.

Johnson, C. (1985). Initial consultation for patients with bulimia and anorexia nervosa. In D. M. Garner & P. E. Garfinkel (Eds.), *Handbook of psychotherapy for anorexia nervosa and bulimia* (pp. 19-51). New York: Guilford.

Kanefield, E. L. (1990). Psychological services at the Julliard School. *Medical Problems of Performing Artists, 5,* 41-44.

Kaplan, L. (1983). Mistakes gifted young people too often make. *Roeper Review, 6,* 73-77.

Kernberg, O. F. (1975). *Borderline conditions and pathological narcissism.* New York: Jason Aronson.

Kernberg, O. F. (1984). Regression in organizational leadership. In M. F. R. K. de Vries (Ed.), *The Irrational executive: Psychoanalytic explorations in management* (pp. 38-66). New York: International University Press.

Keys, A., Brozek, J., Henschel, A., Mickelsen, O., & Taylor, H. L. (1950). *The biology of human starvation* (Vols. 1-2). Minneapolis: University of Minnesota Press.

Kirkendall, D. T., & Calabrese, L. H. (1983). Physiologic aspects of dance. *Clinics in Sports Medicine, 2,* 525-537.

Klint, K. A., & Weiss, M. R. (1986). Dropping in and out: Participation motives of current and former youth gymnasts. *Canadian Journal Applied Sport Science, 11,* 106-114.

Kogan, N. (1994). On aesthetics and its origins: Some psychobiological and evolutionary considerations. *Social Research, 61,* 139-165.

Kogan, N. (1995, September). Motivational and personality patterns in performing artists. Paper presented at the Fifth Annual Esther Katz Rosen Symposium on the Psychological Development of Giften Children, Lawrence, Kansas.

Kohut, H. (1971). *The analysis of the self: A systematic approach to the psychoanalytic treatment of narcissistic personality disorders.* New York: International Universities Press.

Kohut, H. (1977). *The restoration of the self.* New York: International Universities Press.

Kreuger, V. M. (1976). A re-evaluation of narcissism. (Doctoral dissertation, Ohio State University, 1976) *Dissertation Abstracts International, 37-05B,* 2512.

Krueger, D. W. (1981). Emotional rehabilitation of the physical rehabilitation patient. *International Journal of Psychiatry in Medicine, 11,* 183-191.

Kruger, L. J., Bernstein, G., & Botman, H. (1995). The relationship between team friendships and burnout among residential counselors. *Journal of Social Psychology, 135,* 191-201.

Kubler-Ross, E. (1975). *Death: The final stage of growth.* Englewood Cliffs, NJ: Prentice-Hall.

Lechner, D. E. (1994). Work hardening and work conditioning interventions: Do they affect disability? *Physical Therapy, 74,* 471-493.

Lehrer, P. M. (1987). A review of the approaches to the management of tension and stage fright in music performance. *Journal of Research in Musical Education, 35,* 143-153.

Lehrer, P. M., Rosen, R. C., Kostis, J. B., & Greenfield, D. (1987). Treating stage fright in musicians: The use of beta blockers. *New Jersey Medicine, 84*(1), 27-33.

Lerman, A. (1979). Narcissism in the physical rehabilitation patient. *American Journal of Psychoanalysis, 39,* 265-272.

Lindner, H. (1990). How to deal with emotional issues upon retirement or termination of practice. In E. A. Margenau (Ed.), *The encyclopedic handbook of private practice.* New York: Gardner.

Lowen, A. (1983). *Narcissism. Denial of the true self.* New York: Collier Macmillan.

Lowenfield, H. (1976). Notes on shamelessness. *Psychoanalytic Quarterly, 45,* 62-72.

Lowman, R. L. (1993). *Counseling and psychotherapy of work dysfunctions.* Washington, DC: American Psychological Association.

Lucas, A. R., Beard, C. M., O'Fallon, W. M., & Kurland, L. T. (1991). 50-Year trends in the incidence of anorexia nervosa in Rochester, Minn: A population-based study. *American Journal of Psychiatry, 148,* 917-922.

Lykken, D. T., McGue, M., Tellegen, A., & Bouchard, T. J., Jr. (1992). Emergenesis. Genetic traits that may not run in families. *American Psychologist, 47,* 1565-1577.

Marchant-Haycox, S. E., & Wilson, G. D. (1992). Personality and stress in performing artists. *Personality and Individual Differences, 13,* 1061-1068.

Maslow, A. H. (1968). *Toward a psychology of being* (2nd ed). Princeton, NJ: Van Nostrand.

Mayfield, B., & Nash, W. R. (1976). Career attitudes of female professors. *Psychological Reports, 39,* 631-634.

McAllister, D. E., & McAllister, W. R. (1967). Incubation of fear: An examination of the concept. *Journal of Experimental Research in Personality, 2,* 180-190.

McFarland, C., & Buehler, R. (1995). Collective self-esteem as a moderator of the frog-pond effect in reactions to performance feedback. *Journal of Personality and Social Psychology, 68,* 1055-1070.

Miller, A. (1990). *The drama of the gifted child.* New York: Basic Books.

Millon, T. (1994). Personality disorders: Conceptual distinctions and classification issues. In P. T. Costa, Jr. & T. A. Widiger (Eds.), *Personality disorders and the five-factor model of personality* (pp. 279-301). Washington, DC: American Psychological Association.

Moir, A., & Jessel, D. (1991). *Brain sex. The real difference between men and women.* New York: Carol Publishing Group.

Morrison, A. P. (1986). Shame, ideal self, and narcissism. In A. P. Morrison (Ed.), *Essential papers on narcissism* (pp. 348-371). New York: New York University Press.

Mostow, E., & Newberry, P. (1975). Work role and depression in women: A comparison of workers and housewives in treatment. *American Journal of Orthopsychiatry, 45,* 538-548.

Mrazek, P. J., & Haggerty, R. J. (Eds.) (1994). *Reducing risks for mental disorders: Frontiers for preventive intervention research.* Washington, DC: National Academy Press.

Nagel, J. J. (1988). In pursuit of perfection: Career choice and performance anxiety in musicians. *Medical Problems of Performing Artists, 3,* 140-145.

Nagel, J. J. (1990). Performance anxiety and the performing musician: A fear of failure or a fear of success? *Medical Problems of Performing Artists, 5,* 37-40.

Nicholas, J. A. (1975). Risk factors, sports medicine and the orthopedic system: An overview. *Journal of Sports Medicine, 3,* 243-259.

Nisbett, R. E. (1972). Eating behavior and obesity in men and animals. *Advances in Psychosomatic Medicine, 7,* 173-193.

Oliver, J. M., & Paull, J. C. (1995). Self-esteem and self-efficacy; perceived parenting and family climate; and depression in university students. *Journal of Clinical Psychology, 51,* 467-481.

Olivier, L. (1982). *Confessions of an actor.* An autobiography. New York: Simon & Shuster.

Osipow, S. H., & Spokane, A. R. (1983). *A manual for measures of occupational stress, strain, and coping.* Columbus, OH: Marathon Consulting and Press.

Oskarsson, H., & Klein, R. H. (1982). Leadership change and organizational regression. *International Journal of Group Psychotherapy, 32,* 145-162.

Ostwald, P., & Avery, M. (1991). Psychiatric problems of performing artists. In R. T. Sataloff, A. G. Brandfonbrener, & R. J. Lederman (Eds.), *Textbook of performing arts medicine* (pp. 319-335). New York: Raven.

Paul, J. P. (1993). Childhood cross-gender behavior and adult homosexuality: The resurgence of biological models of sexuality. *Journal of Homosexuality, 24*(3/4), 41-54.

Pezenick, D. (1992). Taking the anxiety out of performance. *Chamber Music, 9*(4), 20-23.

Phelps, L., Andrea, R., Rizzo, F. G., Johnston, L., & Main, C. M. (1993). Prevalence of self-induced vomiting and laxative/medication abuse among female adolescents: A longitudinal study. *International Journal of Eating Disorders, 14,* 375-378.

Phillips, E. M. (1991). Acting as an insecure occupation: The flipside of stardom. In G. D. Wilson (Ed.), *Psychology and performing arts* (pp. 133-142). Amsterdam: Swets & Zeitlinger.

Plaut, E.A. (1988). Psychotherapy of performance anxiety. *Medical Problems of Performing Artists, 3,* 113-118.

Press, A. (1992, August 10). Old too soon, wise too late? *Newsweek, 120,* 22-24.

Pruett, K.D. (1991). Psychological aspects of the development of exceptional young performers and prodigies. In R. T. Sataloff, A. G. Brandfonbrener, & R.J. Lederman (Eds.), *Textbook of performing arts medicine* (pp. 337-349). New York: Raven.

Pulver, S. E. (1970). Narcissism: The term and the concept. *Journal of the American Psychoanalytic Association, 18,* 319-341.

Raeburn, S. D. (1987). Occupational stress and coping in a sample of rock musicians. *Medical Problems of Performing Artists, 2,* 41-48.

Reciniello, S. (1991). Toward an understanding of the performing artist: A study of actors and dancers. In G. D. Wilson (Ed.), *Psychology and performing arts* (pp. 95-122). Amsterdam: Swets & Zeitlinger.

Richter, A. L., Reaves, M. G., Deaver, H. D., & Lacy, S. G. (1982). Social stereotypes as a variable in egocentricism. *Journal of Early Adolescence, 2,* 173-183.

Roberts, G. C., & Treasure, D. C. (1993). Children in sport. *Sport Science Review, 1*(2), 46-64.

Robertson, P. (1994). *The Guinness book of movie facts and feats.* New York: Abbeville, p. 115.

Robson, B. E., & Gitev, M. (1991a). In search of perfection. *Medical Problems of Performing Artists, 6,* 15-20.

Robson, B. E., & Gitev, M. (1991b). Where has Gypsy Rose Lee's mother gone? Or the family background of talented students under psychiatric care. *Medical Problems of Performing Artists, 6,* 98-102.

Ronningstam, E., Gunderson, J., & Lyons, M. (1995). Changes in pathological narcissism. *American Journal of Psychiatry 152*(2), 253-257.

Rook, K. S. (1987). Social support versus companionship: Effects on life stress, loneliness, and evaluations by others. *Journal of Personality and Social Psychology, 52,* 1132-1147.

Schantz, P. G., & Astrand, P. (1984). Physiological characteristics of classical ballet. *Medicine and Science in Sports and Exercise, 16,* 472-476.

Schnitt, J. M., Schnitt, D., & Del A'Une, W. (1986). Anorexia nervosa or thinness in modern dance students: Comparison with ballerinas. *Annals of Sports Medicine, 3,* 9-13.

Shelov, S., & Kelly, J. (1991). *Raising your type A child.* New York: Pocket Books.

Silverstein, B., Peterson, B., Perdue, L., & Kelly, E. (1986). The role of the mass media in promoting a thin standard of bodily attractiveness for women. *Sex Roles, 14,* 519-532.

Silverstone, P. H. (1990). Low self-esteem in eating disordered patients in the absence of depression. *Psychological Reports, 67,* 276-278.

Smith, R. E., & Smoll, F. L. (1990). Sport performance anxiety. In H. Leitenberg (Ed.), *Handbook of social and evaluation anxiety* (pp. 417-454). New York: Plenum.

Solomon, R. (1985). Creativity and normal narcissism. *Journal of Creative Behavior, 19,* 47-55.

Spielberger, C. D. (1975). Anxiety: State-trait process. In C. D. Spielberger & I. G. Sarason (Eds.), *Stress and anxiety* (Vol. 1, pp. 115-143). New York: Hemisphere.

Srivastava, A. K. (1989). Moderating effect of n-self actualization on the relationship of role stress with job anxiety. *Psychological Studies, 34,* 106-109.

Stearns, S., & VanderWoude, A. (1991). Musical talent among first-degree relatives of university students majoring, or not majoring, in instrumental or vocal music. Unpublished student research report, University of Minnesota, Department of Psychology, Minneapolis.

Steptoe, A., & Fidler, H. (1987). Stage fright in orchestral musicians: A study of cognitive and behavioral strategies in performance anxiety. *British Journal of Psychology, 78,* 241-249.

Stolorow, R. D. (1975). Toward a functional definition of narcissism. *International Journal of Psycho-analysis, 56,* 179-185.

Stricker, G., & Gold, J. R. (Eds.) (1993). *The comprehensive handbook of psychotherapy integration.* New York: Plenum.

Stunkard, A. J., Harris, J. R., Pederson, N. L., & McClearn, G. E. (1990). The body-mass index of twins who have been reared apart. *New England Journal of Medicine, 322,* 1483-1487.

Stunkard, A. J., Sorensen, T. I. A., Hanis, C., Teasdale, T. W., Chakraborty, R., Schull, W. J., & Schulsinger, F. (1986). An adoption study of human obesity. *New England Journal of Medicine, 314,* 193-198.

Swift, W. J., & Stern, S. (1982). The psychodynamic diversity of anorexia nervosa. *International Journal of Eating Disorders, 2*(1), 17-35.

Tatelbaum, J. (1980). *The Courage to Grieve.* New York: Lippincott & Crowell.

Taylor, S. E., & Brown, J. D. (1988). Illusion and well-being: A social psychological perspective on mental health. *Psychological Bulletin, 103,* 193-210.

Terry, D. J., & Kearnes, M. (1993). Effects of an audience on the task performance of subjects with high and low self-esteem. *Personality and Individual Differences, 15,* 137-145.

Thiel, A., & Schussler, G. (1995). Obsessive-compulsive symptoms in narcissistic self-system disturbances: An exemplary study in anorexia and bulimia nervosa. *Journal of Psychosomatic Medicine and Psychoanalysis, 41,* 60-76.

Tofler, I. R., Stryer, B. K., Micheli, L. J., & Herman, L. R. (1996). Physical and emotional problems of elite gymnasts. *The New England Journal of Medicine, 335,* 281-283.

Tomlinson-Keasey, C., & Little, T. D. (1990). Predicting educational attainment, occupational achievement, intellectual skill, and personal adjustment among gifted men and women. *Journal of Educational Psychology, 82,* 442-455.

United States Bureau of the Census (1990). Earnings by occupation and education (SSTF:22A). Washington, D.C: Government Printing Office.

Van Dyke, J. (1996). Gender and success in the American dance world. *Women's Studies International Forum, 19,* 535-543.

Vincent, L. M. (1989). *Competing with the sylph: The quest for the perfect dance body* (2nd ed.). Princeton, NJ: Princeton Book Co.

Walters, E. E., & Kendler, K. S. (1995). Anorexia nervosa and anorexic-like syndromes in a population-based female twin sample. *American Journal of Psychiatry, 152,* 64-71.

Wardle, J., & Marsland, L. (1990). Adolescent concerns about weight and eating: A social-developmental perspective. *Journal of Psychosomatic Research, 34,* 377-391.

Warren, M. P., Brooks-Gunn, J., Hamilton, L. H., Warren, L. F., & Hamilton, W. G. (1986). Scoliosis and fractures in young ballet dancers: Relation to delayed menarche and secondary amenorrhea. *New England Journal of Medicine, 314,* 1348-1353.

Watson, P. J., Hickman, S. E., Morris, R. J., Milliron, J. T., & Whiting, L. (1995). Narcissism, self-esteem, and parental nurturance. *Journal of Psychology, 129,* 61-73.

Winner, E. (1996). *Gifted children: Myths and realities.* New York: Basic.

Winnicott, D. W. (1965). *The maturational processes and the facilitating environment.* New York: International Universities Press.

Winter, R. B. (1986). Adolescent idiopathic scoliosis. *New England Journal of Medicine, 314,* 1379-1380.

Wolfe, M. L. (1989). Correlates of adaptive and maladaptive musical performance anxiety. *Medical Problems of Performing Artists, 4,* 49-56.

# Author Index

# Subject Index

## ABOUT THE AUTHOR

Linda H. Hamilton, Ph.D., is a clinical psychologist who previously danced with the New York City Ballet. While still a performer, she went to college full-time and got her bachelor's degree from Fordham University in 1984. She then went on to four years of graduate work at Adelphi University, retiring from dance in 1988. Dr. Hamilton received her doctorate in Clinical Psychology in 1989. Her private practice is devoted to the treatment of performing artists. She is also a regular consultant at the School of American Ballet and the Alvin Ailey American Dance Center; the author of numerous professional papers on relevant topics for performers, such as eating disorders, performance anxiety, and problems with career transition; and the monthly advice columnist for *Dance Magazine*, which has more than 230,000 readers. Her first book, *The Person Behind the Mask: A Guide to Performing Arts Psychology* (1997; Ablex Publishing Corp.) is the first of its kind to take a psychoeducational approach to the prevention and treatment of occupational stress in the performing arts. Her second book, *Advice for Dancers* (1998; Jossey-Bass Inc.), is directed specifically toward the dance community. In honor of her leadership role in performing arts psychology, Dr. Hamilton's work is featured in a documentary by European Media Support called "A Vision to Heal." Her biography is also in the *Marquis Who's Who of American Women*.

Lightning Source UK Ltd.
Milton Keynes UK
UKHW02f0649220518

323002UK00019B/530/P